Start Programming with Python
First Edition
James Kelley

Register Your Copy

If you email me your comments on the book or just say, "Hey, I bought your book.", as I develop material I will forward it to you. Lesson Plans, Projects, additional chapters, quiz questions, videos, are all in the various stages of development. Help me keep your book current and useful in the classroom.

I promise I will not sell or give your email address or distribute it, or sell it. It will only be used for me to contact you about new material.

My email address is: jkelley@beach-teach.com

My web site is: http://www.beach-teach.com

INTRODUCTION

For years, I have been teaching a course that introduces Python programming. I decided to put my notes on paper in a form that would serve as a text for the lessons of the course, in the order and the way I teach.

I have had success with my approach and I hope all who use this in their classes or for their own self study, find it worthwhile.

As a user and proponent of Open Source Software, this book was written in its entirety using Apache OpenOffice.org. I used Apache OpenOffice Writer to convert it to a PDF for distribution. The book was written on Windows 10, Mac OS/X, and Ubuntu platforms.

FOR THE INSTRUCTOR:

One of the most frustrating parts of teaching computer related subjects is the books. There are many good books on many subjects. However, I find that for some courses I don't need 24 chapters on a topic that force my instruction into that chapter pattern or sequence. Often I would like a few chapters or even sections from a book, arranged in my sequence, and supplemented by my notes to create a lesson or part of a course.

Python textbooks available are many and varied, for the most part quite good. But, I just needed a few basic lessons to allow me to introduce Computer Studies majors to the basic concepts of Python programming. Also, I am fighting the tendency to teach the way I learned, with long laborious lectures on theory. I find that today's student suffers from what I call "The Sesame Street Syndrome". That is learning in 5 to 10 minute segments in an entertaining way. So, now we must adjust to the new paradigm of teaching and learning. I began this work in an attempt to match this learning pattern. Small segments of lessons with lots of hands on activities.

FOR THE STUDENT:

I teach at a small community college that has kept tuition low. We serve a rural community and most of our students, as in other community colleges are on some type of financial aid. One day in the bookstore I totaled up the cost of two books for a course I was teaching and found that the books cost more than the tuition. No wonder I had students that shared a book or worse yet, did not purchase the book. Those books were not that good that they were worth more than thirteen weeks of instruction. Yes, they had a test bank (often with mistakes), they had the usual tiresome PowerPoint slides (often with mistakes), an instructor manual that, somehow, never fit the way I teach the course and some data files that went with the lab exercises (most I never used). All packed in the book and a CD.

SUPPLEMENTS:

The web page www.beach-teach.com contains supplements to this book. This way I can provide updates to the material on a moments notice. We are teaching in a field where change is good, frequent and where printed copy does not stand the test of time. Test banks while nice, often leave the instructor explaining why a question was wrong. Sometimes I have found that I agree with the student and have no

rationale as to why the test bank had a different answer. So, don't expect big
fancy test banks. Perhaps some questions that I use in my classes but in a format
the instructor can modify to their own satisfaction. Programming Exercises as I
come up with new material are included in the supplemental web page. Once again,
use what you like or make your own. Not very big on PowerPoint slides, why?
Students usually sleep through them and then want to print them out. If you really
need them, make your own as you prepare your lesson. Better yet, use CamStudio or
Jing (for free) to create a short lesson. Use YouTube and make a movie and post it
to make a point. Students like this as they can go to the video as many times as
they need to grasp the information.   Go to www.beach-teach.com for Python Files,
Screenshots and other course information.

SUMMARY

I am a computer programmer who turned teacher. I see a need in my own classroom
for a text with lots of examples that take a student through creating Python
programs, step by step. Hands on is the way to learn programming and this text is
designed to facilitate the students hands on experience. This text gives the
theory in text for reference or reading, then examples written to lead a student
through practicing the theory with step by step examples. So, here is my attempt
to teach Python Programming, Step-by-Step.

Start Programming with Python

Table of Contents

Introduction to Python

Python was created in the Netherlands, around 1990 by Guido von Rossum. The source code for Python is available under the GNU General Public License (GPL). The official Python web site is: http://www.python.org

The documentation can be obtained from the Python site. It is available in PDF, HTML and PostScript formats. Http://www.python.org/doc/

Python is an ideal object oriented programming language for the beginner. Not only is it easy to learn but the code is easy to read which makes it easy to understand. It comes with a rich library of standard functions. It runs on most hardware platforms and supports databases, and GUI programming.

It is an interpreted language which means there is no compile procedure to create executable code. Python compiles each instruction as it is executed. This allows the programmer to enter and test each line independently or put all of the commands in a text file and execute them as a script file.

In the following lessons we will look at running Python instructions from the command line in terminal mode, and from the Python IDLE editor. We will also learn how to create script files and run these script files rather that type a line, execute it then type the next line and execute it and so on. The script files let the programmer write the complete program and then execute it as a single unit.

Chapters 8 and 9 go over the basics of the Graphical User Interface (GUI) called Tk using the Tkinter interface environment. Create windows and place graphics, text, and other widgets to display information on the window and obtain information entered by the user.

This book was designed to teach the beginner how to write simple programs using Python. The best way to use this book is to go over each chapter, do all the examples and make them work. Then do the quiz. Finally do all of the exercises at the end of each lesson. Not only do them but experiment with them. Make all the changes you can think of, try variations of instructions to see how they affect the outcome.

Start Programming with Python

Lesson 1 - Basics of Python

Objectives:

       Define interpreted programming language.
       Run Python from the command line in terminal mode.
       Run Python programs from IDLE.
       Install Python on Windows, Linux and MAC.

1.0 Overview of Python

Python is the creation of Guido van Rossum who still monitors changes to the Python programming language. Python is an interpreted language, this means that it is not compiled and stored but each instruction is compiled as it is encountered. This makes Python a simple, easy to use language. There are no braces {} for blocks of code. Colons and white space define blocks of code.

1.1 IDLE - The Integrated Development Environment.

IDLE is the Python IDE built with the tkinter GUI toolkit. IDLE has the following features:

- coded in 100% pure Python, using the tkinter GUI toolkit
- cross-platform: works on Windows and Unix
- multi-window text editor with multiple undo, Python colorizing and many other features, e.g. smart indent and call tips
- Python shell window (a.k.a. interactive interpreter)
- debugger (not complete, but you can set breakpoints, view and step)

In this course we will look at running from the command line as well as from the IDLE application. We have selected version 2.7 as it is more widely used than the newer version 3.0. Some of the code examples will not run in version 3.0 so for compatibility issues, download version 2.7.

1.2 Installing Python

The tutorial examples were tested Using Ubuntu 11.10 and Python 2.7. Python runs on Linux, Windows and MAC OS/X. Python comes pre-installed on MAC OS/X and Ubuntu. It is a download for Windows from the Python site. There are different IDEs for each different platform. I use IDLE for Ubuntu 11.10 and Python 2.7.

1.3 Using Python - Command Line

Python may be run from the command line or one of several IDE's. In this lesson we will look at both ways. In subsequent lessons we will explore running Python from

.py files. First we will look at running from the command line.

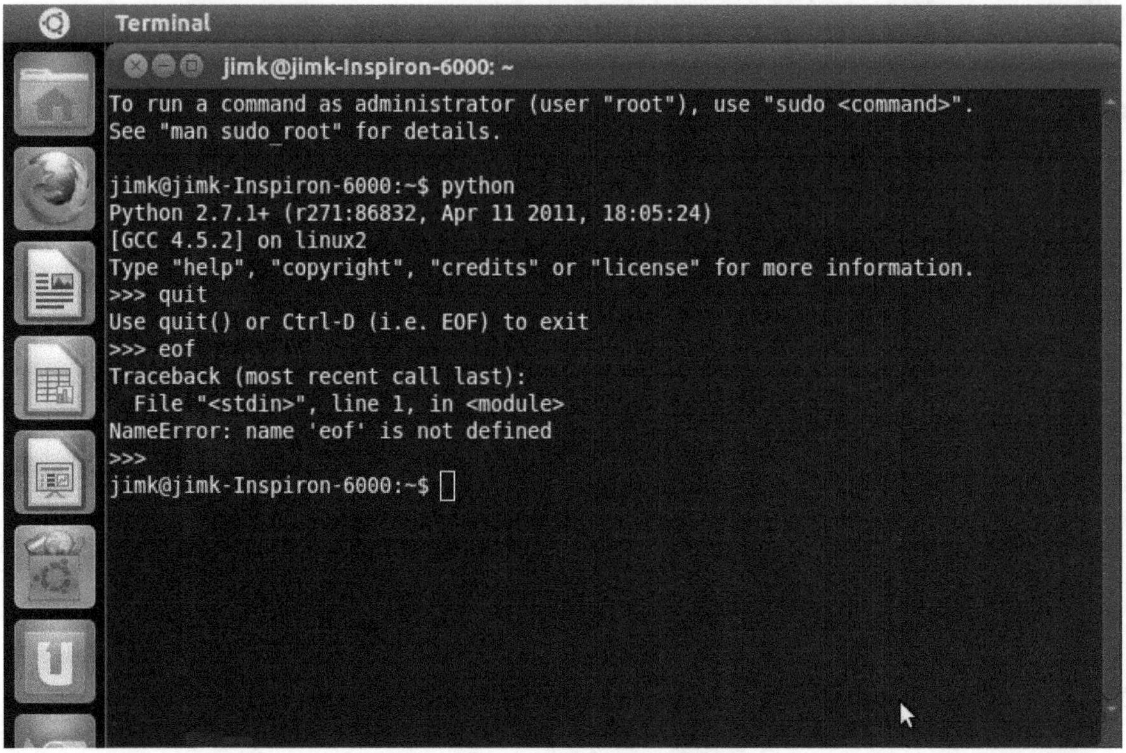

Figure 1.3.1

At the prompt type: python
Then Press the ENTER Key.
When you see the >>> prompt, you can begin to type your commands.

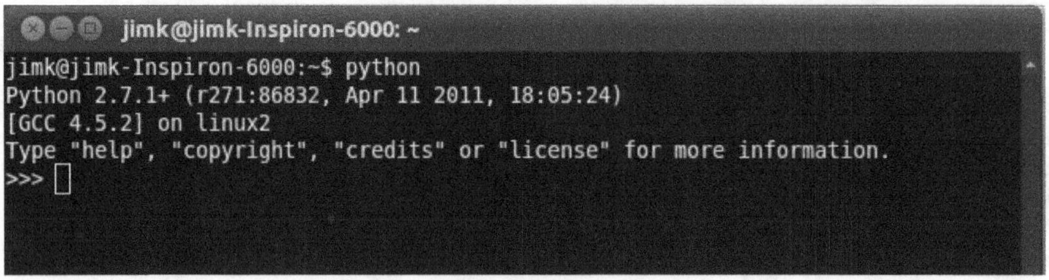

Figure 1.3.2

Type the command after the >>> press enter when complete.
Type Quit or Ctrl+D to exit Python.

Now lets do some experimentation with command line Python:
Go to terminal mode
At the # prompt type python
the >>> indicate python is ready to accept commands

Type the following:

```
print "Hello, World!"
```

GREAT! Now you are a Python programmer.

Here is another way to do the same thing.

```
greet = "Hello, World!"
print greet
```

See, just like the first one. We will explain what happened in later lessons.

1.4 Using Python - IDLE

Python has several IDE products, the one we will examine is called IDLE. IDLE is one of the better IDE products for Python. To access IDLE find the Icon and click. You should see the window shown in Figure 1.4.1.

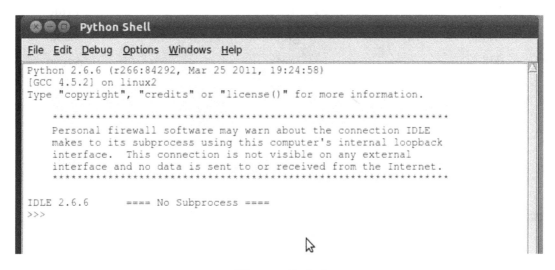

Figure 1.4.1

At the >>> prompt you can begin typing your Python program. Practice using IDLE with the programs we used in Lesson 1.3.

Explore the menu items at the top for testing and running.

1.5 Python Identifiers

An Identifier is a name that is used to identify a function, module, class, variable, or any other Pyghon object. Python is a class sensitive programming language. The word Source and source are seen by Python as two different words.

A Python identifier starts with an uppercase or lowercase letter or an underscore. This is followed by zero or more letters and/or numbers in any combination.

The following is a list of rules for naming identifiers in Python.

- Class names start with an uppercase letter and all other identifiers start with a lowercase letter.

9

- Starting an identifier with a single underscore (_) indicates that the identifier is intended to be private.
- **Starting an identifier with a double underscore (__) indicates that the identifier is intended to be strongly private.**
- **If the identifier also ends with two trailing underscores, the identifer is a language defined special name**

1.6 Python Reserved Words

There are some words that may not be used as constant, variable or any other identifier names.

and	exec	not
assert	finally	or
break	for	pass
class	from	print
continue	global	raise
def	if	return
del	import	try
elif	in	while
else	is	with
except	lambda	yield

1.7 Summary

Python is a simple, easy to use programming language. Python is an interpreted language, each instruction is compiled as it is run. Unlike a compiled language in which all instructions are converted to object code and stored to be run from an executable file. Python is a free download available for Windows, Linux or Mac OS/X. There are two current versions of Python, Version 2.7 and 3.0.

Python may be run either from the command line, from one of several Integrated Development Environments (IDE) or from a stored script file. IDLE is the IDE available for both Windows and Linux.

Lesson 1 - Quiz

1. _____ is a Python IDE
a. PHP
b. Tkinter
c. IDLE
d. QUIZ

2. Python scripts can be written and run on:
a. Windows
b. Mac OS/X
c. Linux
d. All

3. Python may be run from the command line.
a. True
b. False

4. The Python command line prompt is:
a. $
b. <<
c. !
d. >>>

5. The command to exit Python is:
a. Quit
b. Ctrl + D
c. Either A or B
d. Neither A or B or C

6. Any English word can be used as an identifiers
a. True
b. False

7. Python allows the ___ special character in an identifier.
a.   @
b. $
c.   &
d.   none of the above

8. An identifier must have at least one letter and one number.
a. True
b. False

9. The word Compute and the word compute are seen as two different words by Python.
a. True
b. False

Lesson 1 - Exercises

Exercise 1.1 - Print your name.

Enter the following code in the Python command line.

```
print "your name goes here"
```

Exercise 1.2 - Add Some Numbers

Enter the following code in the Python command line.

```
print 8 + 5 * 2
```

Exercise 1.3 - No Calculation

Enter the following code in the Python command line.

```
print "8 + 5 * 2"
```

Exercise 1.4 - First plus Last

Enter the following code in the Python command line.

```
print "Abraham" + " " + "Lincoln"
```

Lesson 2 - Python Programming

Objectives:

Define the term variable.
List the rules for naming variables.
Explain the escape character.
Write a variable statement.
Print the contents of a variable.
Write user input statements.
Compute answers using arithmetic operators.
Manipulate string values.

2.1 Hello, World!

The obligatory Hello, World! Program. Just about every programming book that has
been written for beginners starts with the "Hello, World!" program. So, in an
effort to stay with tradition we too will start with this programming standard. The
first line places the string literal "Hello, World!" in the variable named message.
The second line prints the contents of the variable message to the screen.

```
>>>message = "Hello, World!"
>>>print message
```

Figure 2.1.1

Do this at the terminal command line and then repeat at the IDLE command line

2.2 Variables

A variable is a storage place in computer memory that can hold a value. The
location can be given a name to make it easier to reference in subsequent code.
Much better than the numerical address that the computer can understand. Python is
not fussy about the type of data you store in a variable, it will take any number
or string value you hand it. This makes Python a "loosely typed" programming
language.

```
avg_temp = 90
print avg_temp
```

```
avg_temp = 98.6
print avg_temp
```

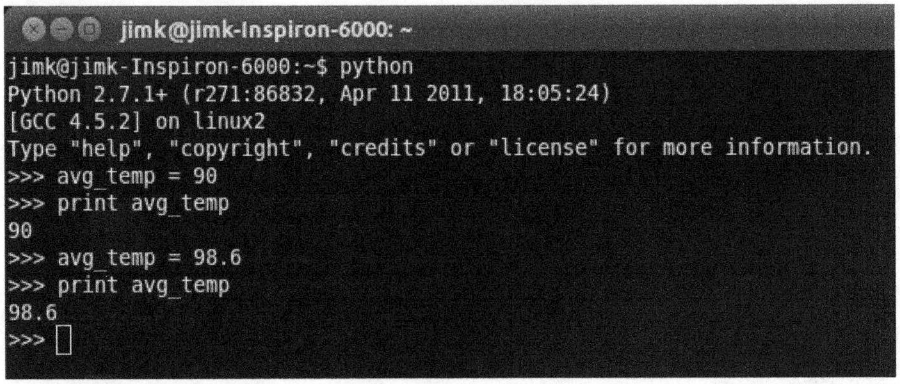

Figure 2.2.1

There are four numerical types in Python.

```
int
long
float
complex
```

You do not have to attach one of these types to a variable. Any variable will accept any of the four data types, even if you load a variable with an int, you can load a float to it the next time you use it.

Naming rules for variables:
- must start with a letter
- contains only letters, digits, and underscore (_)
- no keywords/reserved words

Strings

```
language = "Python"
language = 'Python'
```

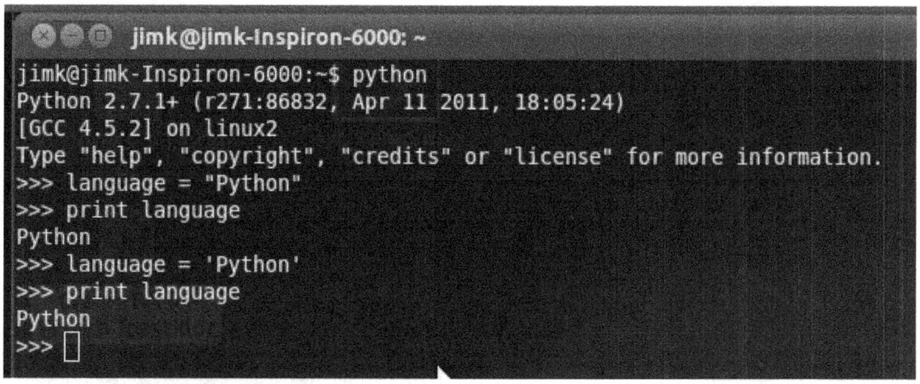
```
jimk@jimk-Inspiron-6000: ~
jimk@jimk-Inspiron-6000:~$ python
Python 2.7.1+ (r271:86832, Apr 11 2011, 18:05:24)
[GCC 4.5.2] on linux2
Type "help", "copyright", "credits" or "license" for more information.
>>> language = "Python"
>>> print language
Python
>>> language = 'Python'
>>> print language
Python
>>>
```

Figure 2.2.2

Single or double quotes are ok.

Data types are no concern to Python variables. You name the variable and then store whatever you want in the variable, integer, floating-point, or string.

```
number = 55
number = 65.87
number = "One Hundred Seventy Five"
```

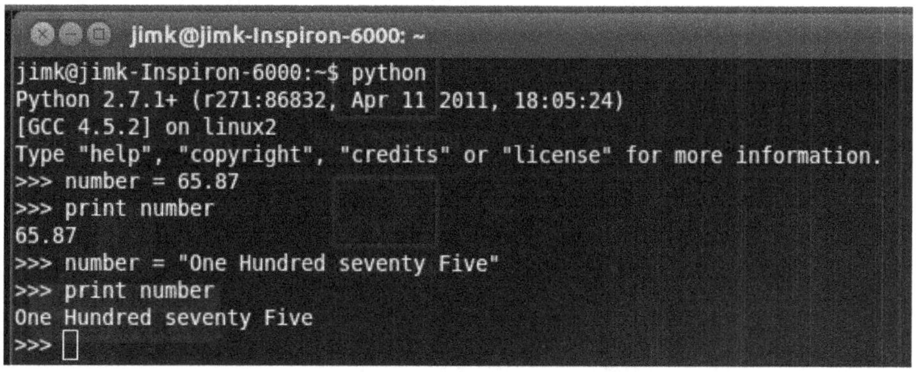
```
jimk@jimk-Inspiron-6000: ~
jimk@jimk-Inspiron-6000:~$ python
Python 2.7.1+ (r271:86832, Apr 11 2011, 18:05:24)
[GCC 4.5.2] on linux2
Type "help", "copyright", "credits" or "license" for more information.
>>> number = 65.87
>>> print number
65.87
>>> number = "One Hundred seventy Five"
>>> print number
One Hundred seventy Five
>>>
```

Figure 2.2.3

2.3 The Escape Character

The "Escape" character allows the programmer to embed symbols like double quotes, tabs, line feeds, etc in strings, store them and then display them. The escape character is the backslash (\\) in front of the character you want to display.

```
quotation = "\"If you are going through hell, keep moving\""
print quotation

data = "one\ttwo\nthree"
print data
```

Figure 2.3.1

Some of the more popular combinations. There are others but these are used quite often.

Backslash + backslash	Prints the backslash
Backslash + doublequotes	Prints doublequotes
Backslash + t	Tabs one tab stop
Backslash + n	Positions the cursor at the beginning of a new line

2.4 User Input - Numbers

Often a program needs to obtain data from the user. Numbers may be requested by the input() function. The syntax of this function is below

<variablename> = input(<prompt>)

The example below will ask the user to "Enter a grade 0 to 100 " and when the user types in a number it will be stored in the variable named "grade".

```
grade = input("Enter a grade 0 to 100 ")
print grade
```

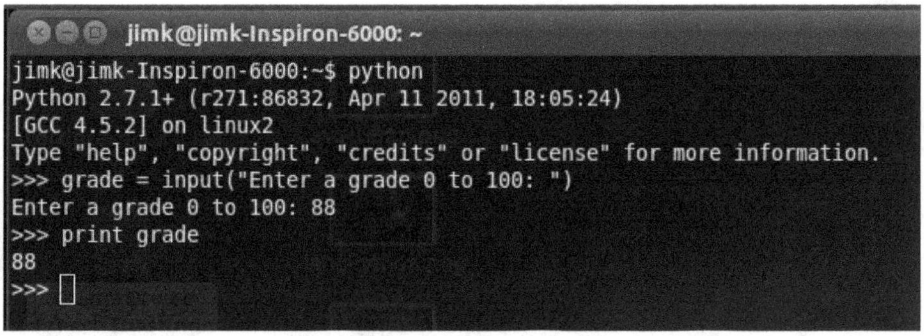

Figure 2.4.1

Enter integers and decimals and they will be printed using the print statement. You can demonstrate an error by entering a string.

2.5 User Input - Strings

Strings may also be entered from the user by using the raw_input() function. The syntax of this function is shown here:

<variablename> = raw_input(<prompt>)

The following example asks the user to "Enter your user name: " and then stores the string entered in the variable names "uname".

uname = raw_input("Enter your User Name: ")
print uname

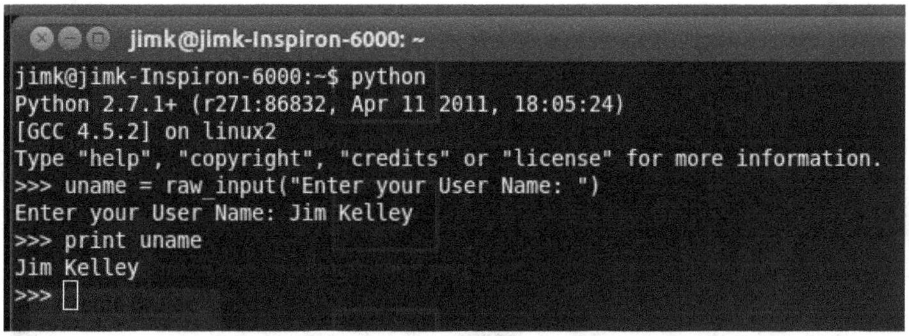

Figure 2.5.1

The program asks for a name, stores it in the variable uname and then prints the name entered stored in uname and displays it.

2.6 Arithmetic

There are six (6) arithmetic operators (+) for addition; (-) for subtraction; (*) for multiplication; (/) for division; (%) for modulus (obtaining the remainder of integer division); and (**) for exponentation. While Python variables do not

17

enforce any rules on the types of data contained in a variable, there are consequences to how data is represented.

```
jimk@jimk-Inspiron-6000: ~
jimk@jimk-Inspiron-6000:~$ python
Python 2.7.1+ (r271:86832, Apr 11 2011, 18:05:24)
[GCC 4.5.2] on linux2
Type "help", "copyright", "credits" or "license" for more information.
>>> num1 = 9
>>> num2 = 4
>>> print num1 + num2
13
>>> print num1 - num2
5
>>> print num1 * num2
36
>>> print num1 / num2
2
>>> print num1 % num2
1
>>> print num1 ** num2
6561
>>>
```

Figure 2.6.1

```
num1 = 9
num2 = 4
print num1 / num2

        vs

num1 = 9.0
num2 = 4.0
print num1 / num2
```

```
jimk@jimk-Inspiron-6000: ~
jimk@jimk-Inspiron-6000:~$ python
Python 2.7.1+ (r271:86832, Apr 11 2011, 18:05:24)
[GCC 4.5.2] on linux2
Type "help", "copyright", "credits" or "license" for more information.
>>> num1 = 9.0
>>> num2 = 4.0
>>> print num1 / num2
2.25
>>> num1 = 9
>>> num2 = 4
>>> print num1 / num2
2
>>>
```

Figure 2.6.2

The first example shows the division of two integers (whole numbers) and the second example the division of two floating-point numbers (numbers with a decimal part).

The next example is an example of integer division and then the same variables used in obtaining the modulus (remainder of integer division).

```
num1 = 9
num2 = 4
print num1 / num2
print num1 % num2
```

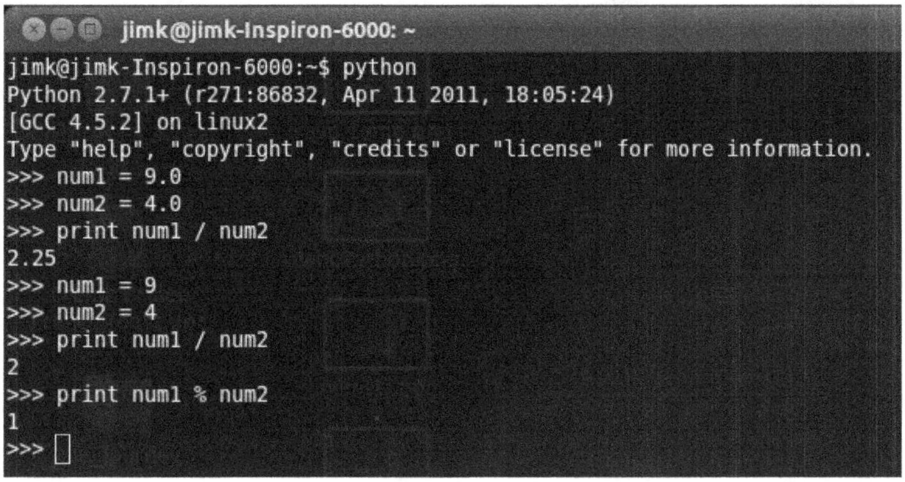

Figure 2.6.3

The last example shows the result of exponentation.

```
print 3**3
```

The double asterisk is the operator for exponentation.

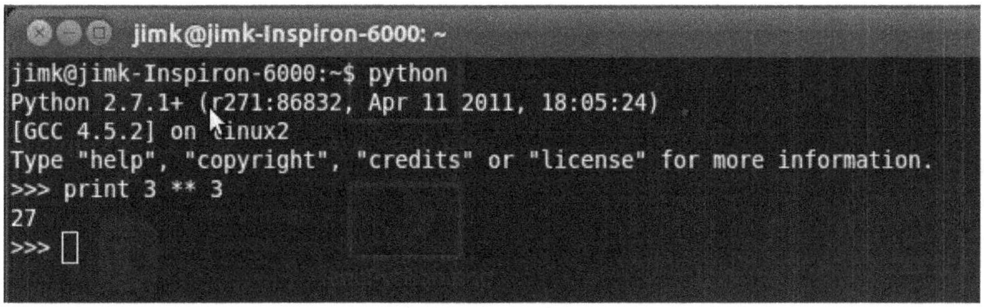

Figure 2.6.4

We can also do arithmetic on the contents of variables and then store the answer in a variable. The new variable can be used in another calculation or printed as needed.

19

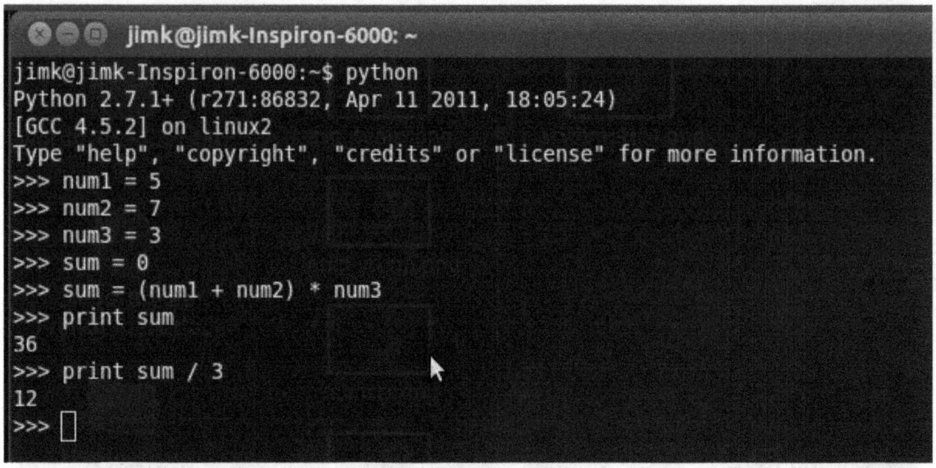

Figure 2.6.5

2.7 String Manipulation

At times it is necessary to concatenate strings of data. For example, if the first name is in one field and the last name in another field and you wish to display the whole name you must concatenate the two fields. In the example below the first name "George" is concatenated with the last name "Washington" and displayed.

```
print "George " +  "Washington
```

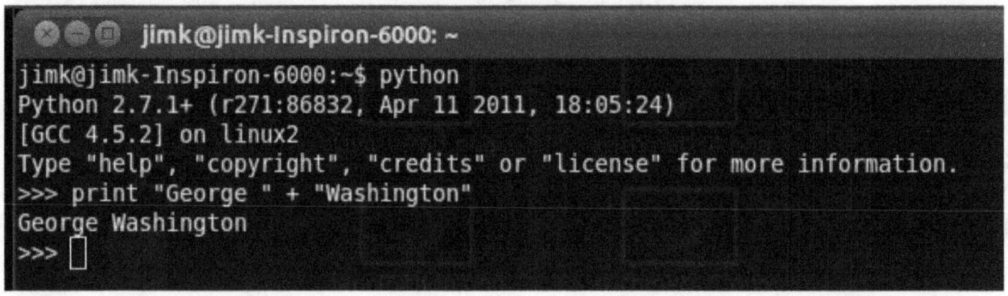

Figure 2.7.1

The next example shows two variables, fname containing "George" and lname containing "Washington". The third statement concatenates fname a space (to separate the two words) and lname and displays the new string on the display.

```
fname = "George"
lname = "Washington"
print fname + " " + lname
```

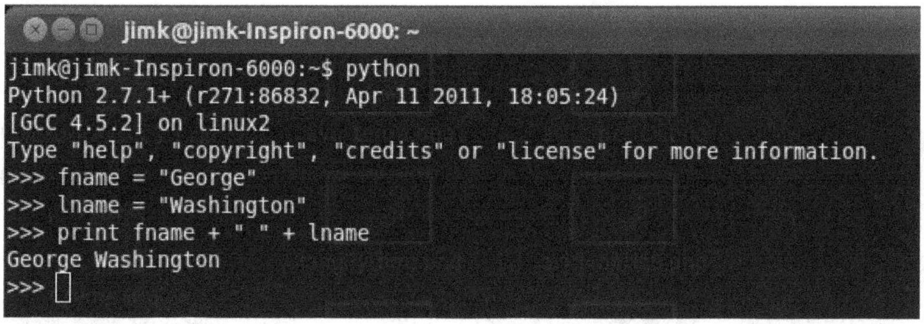

Figure 2.7.2

There are also a series of functions that help allow the manipulation of strings. One of these functions allow the program to determine how many characters are in the string. The example below sets a string in the variable named "phrase" and then displays the number of characters in the string using the len() function.

```
phrase =  "\"A few good men\""
print len(phrase)
```

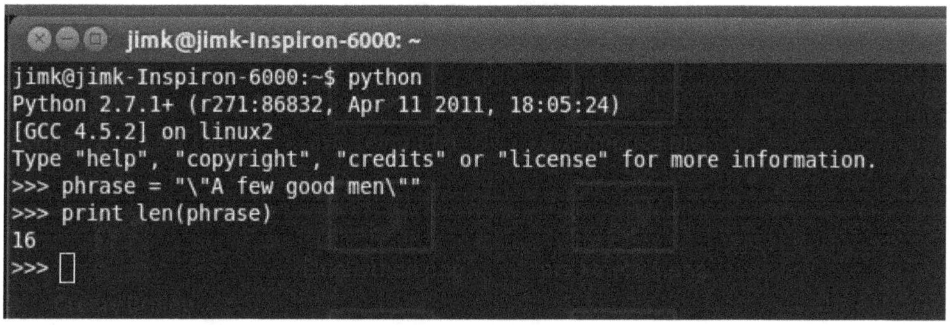

Figure 2.7.3

Some other string functions to explore are:

```
phrase.replace("good", "bad")
```
examines the string named text and replaces all instances of "good" with "bad"
```
phrase.isupper()
```
examines the string in the variable phrase and returns "true" if all characters in the string are uppercase.
```
phrase.islower()
```
examines the string in the variable phrase and returns "true" if all characters in the string are lower case.
```
phrase.upper()
```
Converts the string in the variable phrase to uppercase.
```
phrase.lower()
```
Converts the string in the variable phrase to lower case.
```
phrase.find('w')
```
examines the string in the variable phrase and returns the location of the first occurrence of the letter 'w' or -1 if no letter found.

There are many other string manipulation functions and methods. They can be researched in the Python documentation.

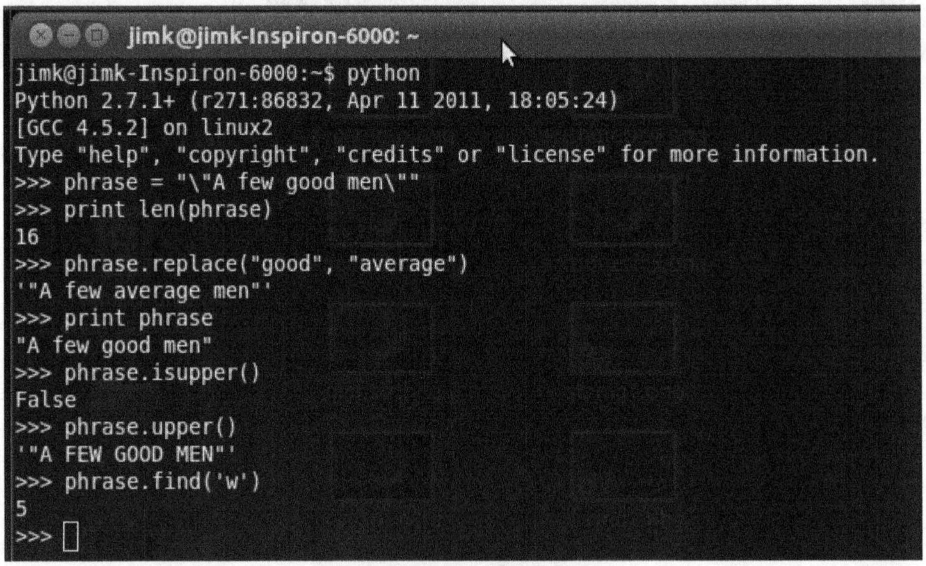

Figure 2.7.4

2.8 Multi-Line Statements

Statements in Python can be spread over more than one line. The continuation character for Python is the line continuation character (\). If a statement is contained by {}, [], or () it does not require a continuation character.

Example:

```
AnnualExpense =      QuarterOneExpense + \
                     QuarterTwoExpense + \
                     QuarterThreeExpense + \
                     QuarterFourExpense

Students = ('John', 'Frederick', 'Symantha', 'Maria',
            'Phillip', 'Barbara', 'Edward')
```

The first example shows four numerical variables summed with the sum stored in the variable named AnnualExpense.

The second example shows seven string values assigned to the identifier Students.

2.9 Summary

Variables are storage places for values, numeric or strings. Each variable has a name to make it easier for the programmer to address the value contained in the storage place. A Python variable can hold any type of data. Unlike many other programming languages, Python is a "loosely typed" programming language where variables can be loaded with one data type and later in the program used for another data type.

Variable names must begin with a letter and can contain letters, digits and the underscore (_) character. A variable name cannot be a reserved word and cannot contain spaces. There are four numerical data types: int; long; float; and complex. String values may be enclosed in either single quotes (') or double quotes("). The quotes at each end of the string must be the same.

Python can perform the six basic arithmetic operations (add, subtract, multiply, divide, modulus, exponentiation) on numbers. It also has the tools and a library of functions to manipulate string data.

Lesson 2 - Quiz

1. A _____ is a storage place in computer memory that can hold a value.
a. element
b. store
c. variable
d. hold

2. Python is not fussy about the type of data you store in a variable. This makes Python a _____ programming language.
a. strictly typed
b. loosely typed
c. tightly typed
d. untyped

3. There are ____ numerical data types in Python.
   a. four
   b. five
   c. six
   d. eight

4. Python accepts either single or double quotes for strings.
a. True
b. False

5. The _____ character allows the programmer to embed symbols like tabs, line feeds, quotes, in strings to store them and display them.
a. escape
b. release
c. insert
d. change

6. The _____ is used to obtain numbers from the user.
a. accept()
b. raw_input()
c. input()
d. innum()

7. The _____ is used to obtain strings from the user.
a. accept()
b. raw_input()
c. input()
d. instring()

8. There are _____ arithmetic operations.
a. three
b. four
c. five
d. six

9. The quotes at each end of a string must be the same.
a. True
b. False

10. There are a series of functions that are used to manipulate strings. Which is NOT a valid function.
a. replace()
b. isupper()
c. islower()
d. revert()

Lesson 2 – Exercises

Exercise 2.1 Assign String Variables.

Enter the following code in the Python command line.

```
message = "Welcome to Python Programming"
print message
```

Exercise 2.2 Assign Number Variables

Enter the following code in the Python command line.

```
num1 = 123456
print num1
```

Exercise 2.3 The Escape Character

Enter the following code in the Python command line.

```
message1 = "\"Fourscore and seven years ago...\""
print message1
```

Exercise 2.4 The Escape Character Advanced

Enter the following code in the Python command line.

```
message1 = "\"Fourscore and seven years ago our forefathers
\nbrought forth on this continent a new nation..\"
\nGettysburg Address\n\tAbraham Lincoln"
print message1
```

Exercise 2.5 Input Numbers

Enter the following code in the Python command line.

```
num1 = input("Enter the first number: ")
num2 = input("Enter the second number: ")
sum = num1 + num2
```

```
print "The sum of the numbers is " + str(sum)
```

Exercise 2.6 Input Strings

Enter the following code in the Python command line.

```
fname = raw_input("Enter your first name: ")
lname = raw_input("Enter your last name: ")
print fname + " " + lname + " is your full name."
```

Exercise 2.7 Integer Division

Enter the following code in the Python command line.

```
num1 = input("Enter the dividend as a whole number: ")
num2 = input("Enter the divisior-must be less than the
dividend: ")
num3 = num1 / num2
num4 = num1 % num2
print "The quotient is " + str(num3)
print "The remainder is " + str(num4)
```

Exercise 2.8 Write your own program

Write a program that prints out a quotation over 5 lines. You may use any quotation but you must indicate the author. You can Google to get a quote. See exercise 2.4 for an example.

Exercise 2.9 Write your own program

Write a program that asks the user for two numbers. Then multiplies the first number by the second number and displays the result.

Lesson 3 - Decisions

Objectives:
- Explain the concept of decisions.
- List the relational operators.
- Write a single sided IF statement.
- Write a IF...ELSE statement.
- Describe Nested IF statements.
- Output formatted strings.
- Create and use one-dimensional arrays.

3.1 Programming Structures

There are three structures in most programming languages. (1) The Sequence Structure - is like the programs we have encountered to this point. The program executes each statement in order from top to bottom. This is great but limits the power of the programs we can create. So let's look at the other structures.

The remaining structures are (2) The Decision Structure - which lets us evaluate an expression and if the expression evaluates to true we take one programming path and if it evaluates false we take a different programming path. The third structure (3) The Repetition Structure - will be studied in the next lesson, allow the program to process instructions repeatedly.

This lesson explores the Decision Structure. A boolean expression (one that can only evaluate to true or false) is examined and a statement or a group of statements is executed if the answer is true and a different statement or group of statements are evaluated if the answer is false.

3.2 Operators

Understanding operators is key in understanding boolean expressions. Boolean expressions are comparisons of two operands and based on the comparison return either an answer of true or false. An example would be 5 > 6 and this would evaluate to false because 5 is NOT greater than 6. Another example 3 == 3, because 3 is equal to 3 this evaluation would return a true. In a program the number operands in our example expressions may be replaced with variables to compare the contents of variables to make decisions.

There are six (6) basic operators for evaluation of boolean expressions (an expression that evaluates to true or false). They are:

<	Less than
<=	Less than or equal to
>	Greater than
>=	Greater than or equal to
==	Equal to
!=	Not equal

A boolean expression is constructed as follows:

[operand1] conditional operator [operand2]

In the evaluation of the expression, operand1 is compared to operand2. The operands may be numeric literals, string literals, variables or combinations.

EXAMPLE:

```
grade = 100
if grade == 100:
    print "Perfection"
```

Figure 3.3.1

Don't forget the colon (:) at the end of the IF statement and you MUST indent the print statement. Python expects an indented statement line after a semicolon. In the example above the print statement in the first attempt was not indented and the resulting error message is shown. The second attempt shows the print statement indented properly.

```
grade = "A"
if grade == "A":
    print  "Excellent"
    grade = 55
if grade < 60:
    print "Failure"
```

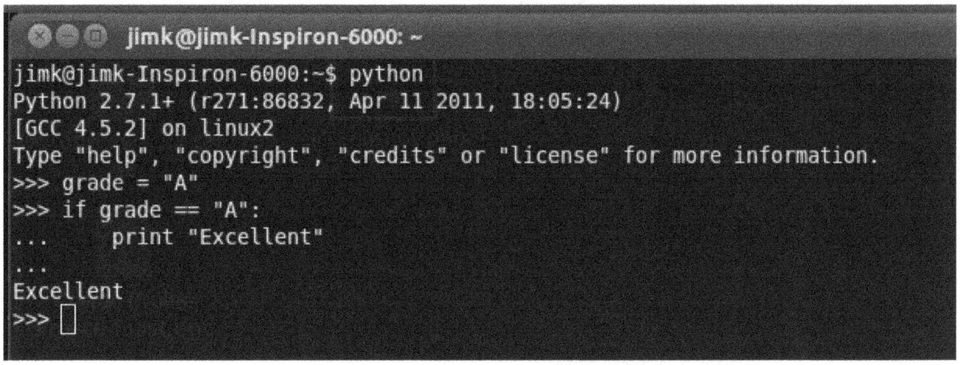

Figure 3.3.2

In this example the variable named "grade" is loaded with the value "A". When the contents of the variable named grade is compared to the string literal "A" the comparison evaluates to true and the print statement will output the message "Excellent". If the expression had evaluated to false, nothing would be printed.

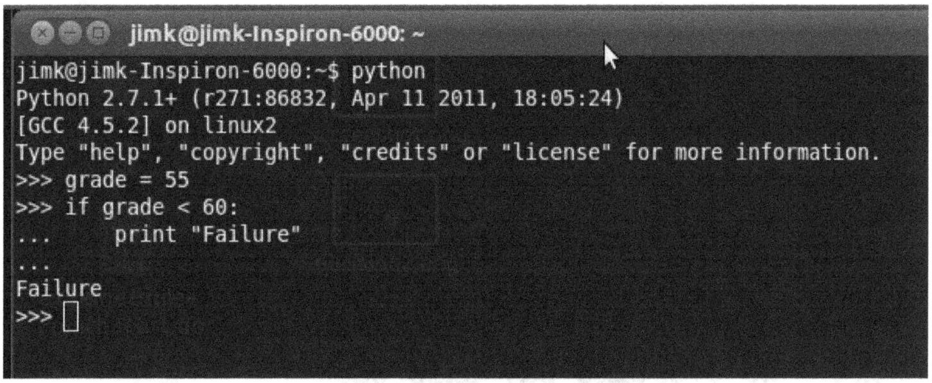

Figure 3.3.3

In this example the variable named "grade" is loaded with the numeric value 55. The contents of the variable named grade is then compared to a numeric literal 60 and the expression evaluates to true and the message "Failure" is output. Note in these comparisons the two operands must be evaluating the same types of data to provide meaningful comparisons. Integers should only be compared to integers, strings to strings, float to float, and so forth. Comparing two different data types will not be able to return an equal comparison.

3.3 The If Statement

The If statement compares operand1 to operand2 and if the comparison results in TRUE, the following statements are executed. If the comparison results in FALSE those statements are skipped.

```
if <condition>:
    <true statements>
```

```
hours = 46
if hours &gt 40:
     otpay = (hours - 40) * (rate * 1.5)
```

In this example the hours variable is compared to the numeric literal 40. If the contents of the variable hours is greater than 40, overtime pay (otpay) is calculated.

3.4 The If...Else Statement

IF...ELSE Statement compares operand1 to operand2 and if the comparison results in TRUE, the statements following are executed up to the else statement and then the program continues after all of the skipped else statements. If the comparison results in FALSE, the true statements are skipped and the statements immediately following the else statement are executed.

```
if <condition>:
     <true statements>
else:
     <false statements>
```

The example shows a program that asks for input of hours worked and evaluates them. If they worked more than 40 hours, a message "You will get overtime pay" will be printed. If they worked 40 or less hours the message "No overtime pay this week" will be printed.

```
hours = input("Enter Hours Worked: ")
if hours > 40:
     print "You will get overtime pay"
else:
     print {"No overtime pay this week"}
```

Key in this example or examine Figure 3.4.1. What happens when you key in 30, 40, 50 hours?

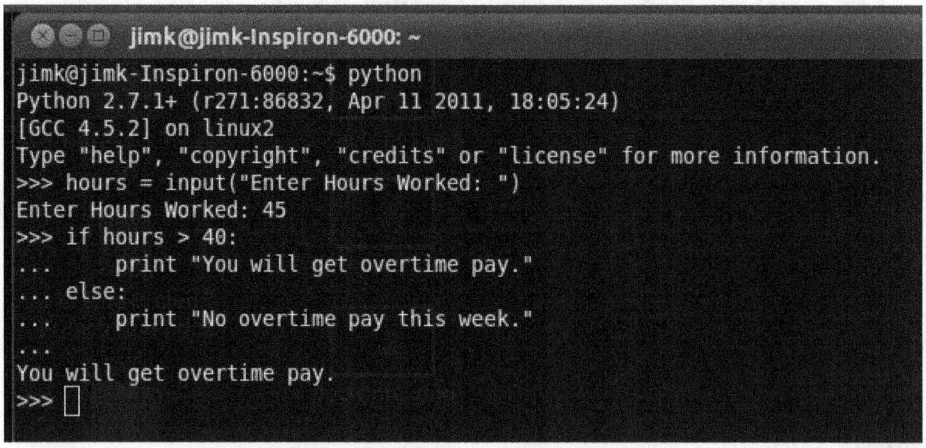

Figure 3.4.1

30

3.5 Nested If Statements

Nested IF statements are when the results of one comparison (true or false) results in another comparison. One of the first questions that pops up is "How many times can you nest statements?" The answer, as many as you need. However, the more you nest the more complex your program becomes and that may be hard to debug or modify. Examine the example below:

```python
age = input("Enter age: ")
reg = input("Enter 1 for registered 2 for not registered")
if age < 18:
    print "Too young to vote"
else:
    if reg == 1:
        print "You may vote"
    else:
        print "You must register to vote"
```

In our example the user is asked for age and if they are registered to vote. If they are under 18 years old, they can't vote. However, if they are 18 or over they can vote if they are registered to vote, so the second comparison is done if the first comparison results in false.

```
jimk@jimk-Inspiron-6000: ~
jimk@jimk-Inspiron-6000:~$ python
Python 2.7.1+ (r271:86832, Apr 11 2011, 18:05:24)
[GCC 4.5.2] on linux2
Type "help", "copyright", "credits" or "license" for more information.
>>> age = input("Enter Age: ")
Enter Age: 21
>>> reg = input("Enter 1 for registered; 2 for not registered: ")
Enter 1 for registered; 2 for not registered: 1
>>> if age < 18:
...     print "Too young to vote"
... else:
...     if reg == 1:
...             print "You may vote"
...     else:
...             print "You must register to vote"
...
You may vote
>>>
```

Figure 3.5.1

3.6 Strings and Functions

Python treats strings and numbers differently. There are a number of functions use to convert numbers to strings, strings to numbers also to convert numbers to other types. We will look at four of the more widely used functions.

str(variablename)

31

```
        converts the variable to a string
eval(variablename)
        converts the variable to a number
int(variablename)
        converts the variable to an integer
float(variablename)
        converts the variable to a floating point number
```

Here are some examples using these functions:

```
sum = 1234
print "The sum is: " + str(sum)
numbr = "54321"
ans = eval(numbr) * 3.14
print ans
num1 = 3.87
print int(num1)
num2 = 49
print float(num2)
```

Figure 3.6.1

3.7 Formatting Strings

```
print "the sum of %d and %d is 6"  % (4, 2)

a = 5
b = 6
print "the sum of %d and %d is %d" % (a, b, a+b)
```

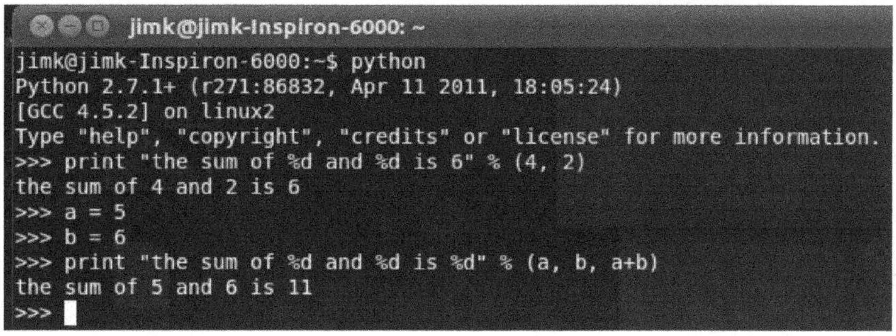

```
jimk@jimk-Inspiron-6000: ~
jimk@jimk-Inspiron-6000:~$ python
Python 2.7.1+ (r271:86832, Apr 11 2011, 18:05:24)
[GCC 4.5.2] on linux2
Type "help", "copyright", "credits" or "license" for more information.
>>> print "the sum of %d and %d is 6" % (4, 2)
the sum of 4 and 2 is 6
>>> a = 5
>>> b = 6
>>> print "the sum of %d and %d is %d" % (a, b, a+b)
the sum of 5 and 6 is 11
>>>
```

Figure 3.7.1

3.8 Multiple Lines

Sometimes it is necessary to split a long statement across several lines or to make a statement fit on a page or make it more readable. Python uses the '\' character to continue a line to the next line.

Here is an example:

```
region_one = 123.45
region_two = 135.79
region_three = 124.68
region_four = 195.32
national_sales = region_one + region_two + \
region_three + region_four
print national_sales
```

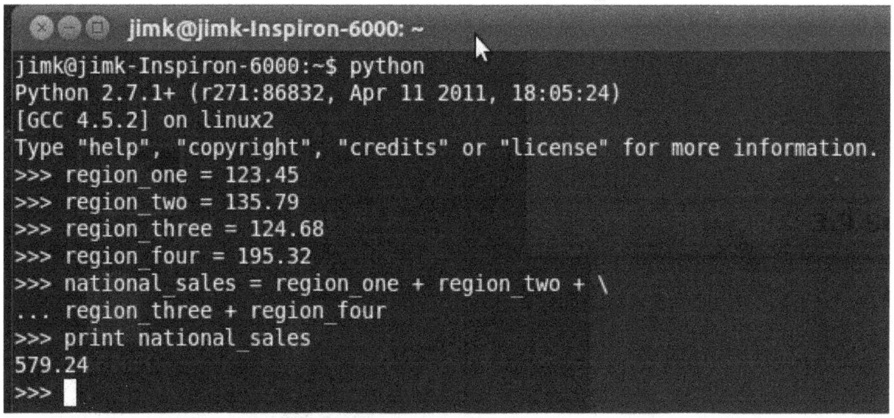

```
jimk@jimk-Inspiron-6000: ~
jimk@jimk-Inspiron-6000:~$ python
Python 2.7.1+ (r271:86832, Apr 11 2011, 18:05:24)
[GCC 4.5.2] on linux2
Type "help", "copyright", "credits" or "license" for more information.
>>> region_one = 123.45
>>> region_two = 135.79
>>> region_three = 124.68
>>> region_four = 195.32
>>> national_sales = region_one + region_two + \
... region_three + region_four
>>> print national_sales
579.24
>>>
```

Figure 3.8.1

3.9 Arrays

Python does not have an array structure. The array structure is a fundamental structure in most programming languages. An array is defined in languages with an array structure as an ordered collection of items of a single type.

Python does have a list structure which is defined as an ordered collection of items of any type. In many ways this is far more flexible and useful than the array structure. You can add and delete elements from the list at any time, most array structures are fixed.

The syntax of the array structure is:

myList={1,2,3,4]

To print the third item in the list use the code:

print myList[3]

Lists may be used when there are a group of related items. In our first example we show the list by defining each element of the list with its own name. This can be burdensome for large lists. For illustrative purposes we are only showing four elements in our list.

```
region_one = 123.45
region_two = 135.79
region_three = 124.68
region_four = 195.32
national_sales = region_one + region_two + \
region_three + region_four
print national_sales
```

Figure 3.9.1

This code adds the four region sales and stores the sum in the variable national_sales. Statements that are contained within parenthesis (), curly brackets {}, or square brackets [] do not require the continuation character. Here is an example:

34

```
regions = ['Northeast', 'MidAtlantic', 'SouthEast',
Midwest', 'SouthWest', 'Northwest']
print regions[2]
```

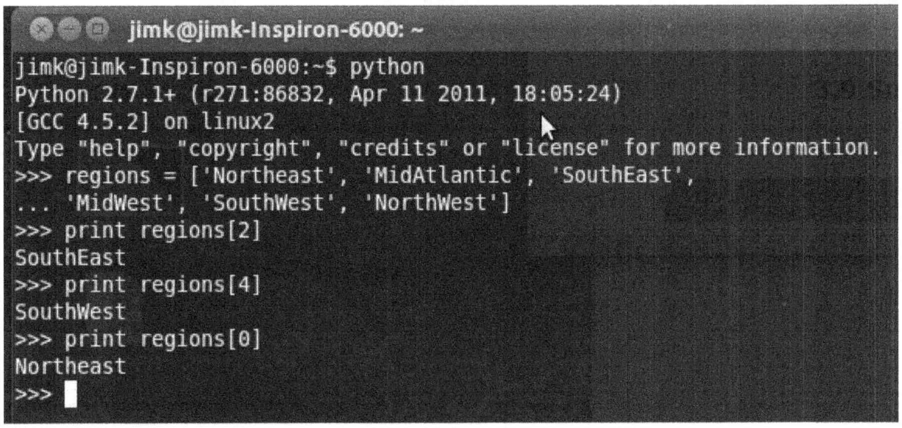

```
jimk@jimk-Inspiron-6000: ~
jimk@jimk-Inspiron-6000:~$ python
Python 2.7.1+ (r271:86832, Apr 11 2011, 18:05:24)
[GCC 4.5.2] on linux2
Type "help", "copyright", "credits" or "license" for more information.
>>> regions = ['Northeast', 'MidAtlantic', 'SouthEast',
... 'MidWest', 'SouthWest', 'NorthWest']
>>> print regions[2]
SouthEast
>>> print regions[4]
SouthWest
>>> print regions[0]
Northeast
>>>
```

Figure 3.9.2

Each element can be addressed by itself by using the array name and the index value of the appropriate element in the array enclosed in square brackets []. Remember, the index value of an array is zero based so the first element is index number zero (0). Note the last example where an invalid index number was entered and the resulting error message.

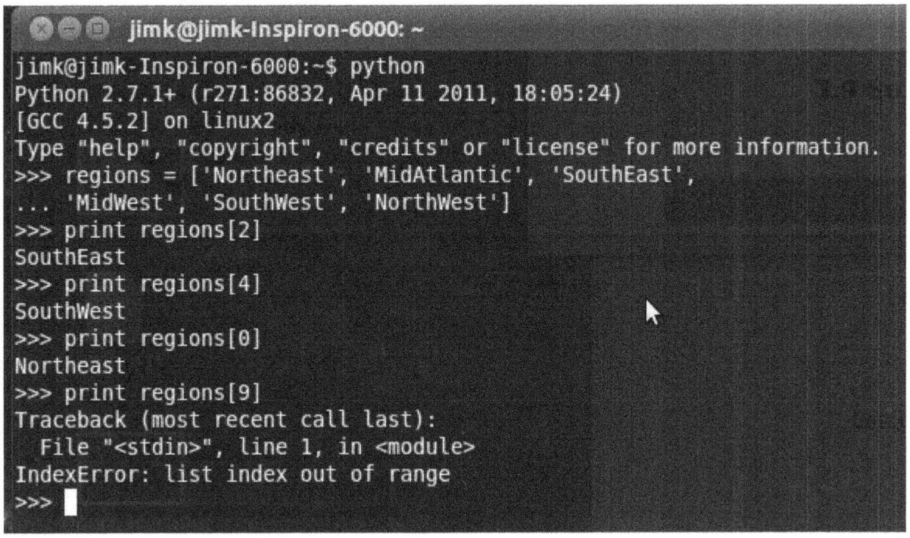

```
jimk@jimk-Inspiron-6000: ~
jimk@jimk-Inspiron-6000:~$ python
Python 2.7.1+ (r271:86832, Apr 11 2011, 18:05:24)
[GCC 4.5.2] on linux2
Type "help", "copyright", "credits" or "license" for more information.
>>> regions = ['Northeast', 'MidAtlantic', 'SouthEast',
... 'MidWest', 'SouthWest', 'NorthWest']
>>> print regions[2]
SouthEast
>>> print regions[4]
SouthWest
>>> print regions[0]
Northeast
>>> print regions[9]
Traceback (most recent call last):
  File "<stdin>", line 1, in <module>
IndexError: list index out of range
>>>
```

Figure 3.9.3

3.10 Summary

This Lesson covered decision making in the Python programming language. Relational operators are the operations that compare two values and produce a boolean (true / false) result. Based on the result an If statement alters the flow of statements. One flow if the result is true and a different flow if the result is false.

To produce human readable output in a form that looks professional requires formatting output strings.

Storing data in a program requires the use of variables. Often, a large amount of data requires storage and to create an array for each would make the program difficult to maintain. In these instances we learn to use arrays.

Lesson 3 - Quiz

1. There are ____ programming structures in most programming languages.
a. two
b. three
c. four
d. eight

2. There are ____ basic operators for evaluation of boolean expressions.
a. two
b. four
c. six
d. eight

3. A _____ expression is an expression that evaluates to true or false.
a. boolean
b. binary
c. dual
d. switch

4. You must put a ____ at the end of an if statement.
a. period
b. comma
c. semicolon
d. colon

5. This statement compares two operands and if the evaluation is true the following, indented, statements are executed, and if evaluation is false those statements are skipped and the program continues.
a. The IF statement
b. The IF...ELSE statement
c. The IF...OK statement
d. Try...Catch

6. _____ statements are when the results of one comparison results in another comparison.
a. Concatenated IF
b. Concurrent IF
c. Normalized IF
d. Nested IF

7. Python treats strings and numbers the same.
a. True
b. False

8. Pyton uses the _____ character to continue a line to the next line.
a. '-'
b. '\'
c. '/'
d. '&'

9. Python does not have an array structure.
a. True
b. False

10. _____ may be used when there are a group of related items.
a. displays
b. relations
c. lists
d. none of the above

Lesson 3 - Exercises

Exercise 3.1 Enter your user name

Enter the following code in the Python command line.

```
uname = raw_input("Enter your user name: ")
if uname != "Sam":
    print "ACCESS DENIED!"
```

Test your program using:

```
ann
sam
Sam
```

Exercise 3.2 Pass or Fail

Enter the following code in the Python command line.

```
grade = input("Enter your grade 0 to 100: ")
if grade < 60:
    print "You did not pass"
else:
    print "You passed"
```

Test your program using:

```
55
97
60
```

Exercise 3.3 Nested If

Enter the following code in the Python command line.

```
balance = input("Enter your bank account balance: ")
if balance < 100:
    print "You will not get any interest"
else:
    if balance >= 100:
    print "You will receive five percent interest"
```

Test your program using:

```
100
97.50
1234.56
```

Lesson 4 - Repetition (Looping)

Objectives:

- Explain the repetition structure.
- Create a loop using the while structure.
- Create a loop using the for structure.
- Use the range function to create a list.
- Use repetition structures to loop through a list.
- Describe nested loops.

4.1 Overview of Repetition

Repetition or Looping is an important concept in programming. These commands unleash the power of the computer instructing the computer to process the same group of instructions over and over until some condition is met. Without these structures, programs that process many items would be huge as the processing instructions would have to be repeated for each unit processed. Then there would be the problem of having to know how many units to be processed each time the program was executed. Therefore programs would only be able to process a fixed number of units and if the number of units varied each time the program was run, there would be problems.

An example would be a payroll processing program. For a small company with less than ten employees, no problem to have a program that would be run once for each person in the company. For a company that may have between 100 and 1000 employees (and the number would change each payroll period) to pay each pay period, this would be a huge problem

Fortunately, we have the repetition structure. We can set up groups of instructions that allow for using the same instructions over and over until some condition exists that will stop the loop to continue processing or exit the program.

4.2 While Loop

The while loop executes as long as the condition evaluated is TRUE. The loop will exit when the condition becomes FALSE. It is important that an instruction in the loop changes the condition or the program will suffer the deadly "infinite loop". Be aware that there is the possibility that the loop statements may never get executed, this is called an "infinite loop". This will happen if the condition tests false before the loop begins. The condition must test true for the instructions in the while loop to be executed.

> **while <condition>**
> **<statements>**

While the "condition" is true execute the statements in the loop. Remember each of the loop statements must be indented to the same level to be considered "in the loop statements block".

Note the colon at end of the while statement. This indicates that there are more statements to follow. The statements that follow must be indented or there will be an error condition shown.

```
counter = 1
while counter <= 3:
    print counter
    counter = counter + 1
    print " "

print counter
```

Figure 4.2.1

Note that there must be an instruction in the loop that changes the condition or we have the dreaded "infinite loop". Also, the last statement in the program is "print counter". Examine the number printed out. What is the rationale for the value printed? It is higher than the last value printed, Why?

4.3 For Loop

The for loop is known as a "Counter Controlled" loop. The for statement initializes the counter variable, sets the evaluation expression and then the value the counter should be incremented or decremented. In Python, the for statement uses the range() function to determine the sequence and the increment value.

```
for <variable> in <sequence>:
    <statements>
```

USING the range() function in a for statement to determine the starting value, the ending value and the increment or decrement value. If no increment or decrement is specified it is assumed that the increment will be +1.

```
range(startvalue, endvalue, increment/decrement)

for count in range(1, 3):
print count
```

In this sample the index variable is named count which is initialized to 1 and will continue until the count reaches 3. It will be incremented by one one each iteration of the loop since no increment or decrement value was specified.

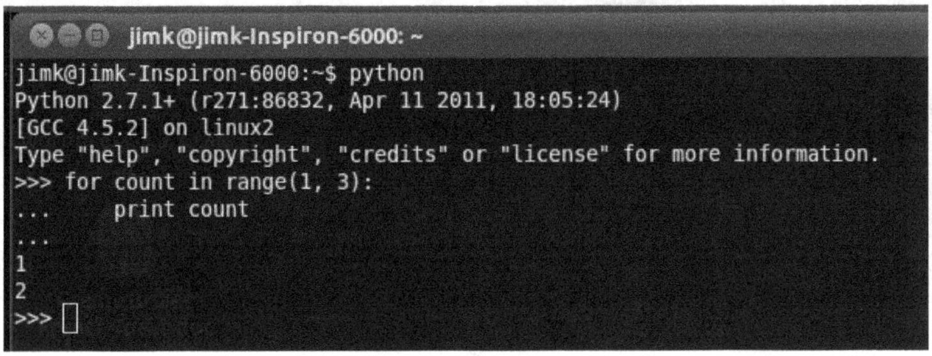

Figure 4.3.1

```
for count in range(0, 10, 2):
print count
```

In this sample the index variable is named count and is initialized to 0 (zero). and will continue until the count reaches 10 (ten). It will be incremented by two on each iteration of the loop because the increment is specified as 2 (two).

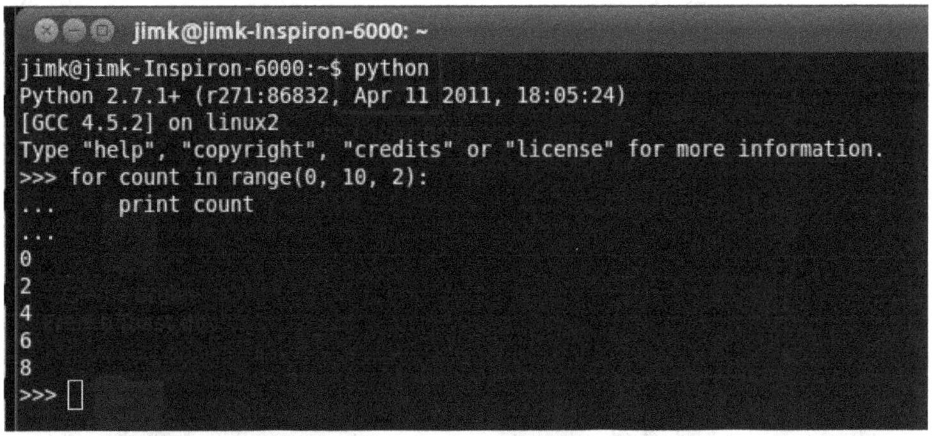

Figure 4.3.2

```
for count in range(10, 0, -2):
print count
```

41

In this sample the index variable is named count and is initialized to 0 (zero). and will continue until the count reaches 10 (ten). It will be decremented by two on each iteration of the loop because the increment is specified as -2 (negative two).

```
jimk@jimk-Inspiron-6000: ~
jimk@jimk-Inspiron-6000:~$ python
Python 2.7.1+ (r271:86832, Apr 11 2011, 18:05:24)
[GCC 4.5.2] on linux2
Type "help", "copyright", "credits" or "license" for more information.
>>> for count in range(10, 0, -2):
...     print count
...
10
8
6
4
2
>>>
```

Figure 4.3.3

The for loop structure uses the range function to determine the scope of the loop. This makes it a valuable tool for accessing the list structure which will be discussed in section 4.5.

4.4 Nested Loops

Nested loops are simply loops within loops. It could be a for loop in another for loop, a while loop within another while loop. Even for loops within while loops or while loops within for loops. How many loops can be nested? There is no limit other than the ability to deal with the code required to generate these nested loops.

```
jimk@jimk-Inspiron-6000: ~
jimk@jimk-Inspiron-6000:~$ python
Python 2.7.1+ (r271:86832, Sep 27 2012, 21:16:52)
[GCC 4.5.2] on linux2
Type "help", "copyright", "credits" or "license" for more information.
>>> for count in range(1, 10):
...     for inside in range(3, 1, -1):
...         print inside
...     print count
...
3
2
1
3
2
2
3
2
3
2
4
3
2
```

Figure 4.4.1

The outer loop is indexed by the variable count. The inside loop is indexed by the variable index. The outer loop counts from 1 to 10 increment by 1. The inside loop counts from 3 to 1 by -1. The 3 and 2 are printed by the inside loop, the following 1 is produced by the outside loop. Then another 3 and 2 from the inside loop followed by a 2 from the outside loop. This pattern continues until the outer loop reaches its limit.

4.5 Break and Continue Commands

If in the course of execution of loop statements, it becomes necessary to exit the loop structure, the programmer has two choices. The programmer can issue a break command or a continue command depending on where the next instruction should execute.

The **break** command transfers control to the program statement immediately following the last statement in the loop structure.

The **continue** command transfers control back to the beginning statement of the loop structure.

4.6 Python Range Function

Python's range function is an example of the use of lists (python's arrays). The range function returns a list of consecutive integers. The range function returns a list of consecutive integers. A list is a sequence of objects. Not only numbers. They are separated by commas and enclosed in brackets. The for statement creates the following list:

```
for i in range(5):
or
for i in {0, 1, 2, 3, 4}:
```

Both examples produce the same results, a list of 0, 1, 2, 3, 4, a list of 5 numbers.

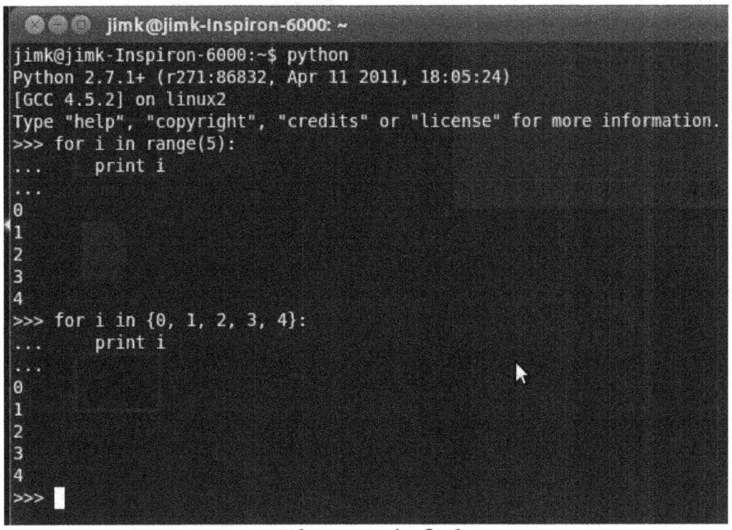

Figure 4.6.1

Example of program printing the contents of a list (array).

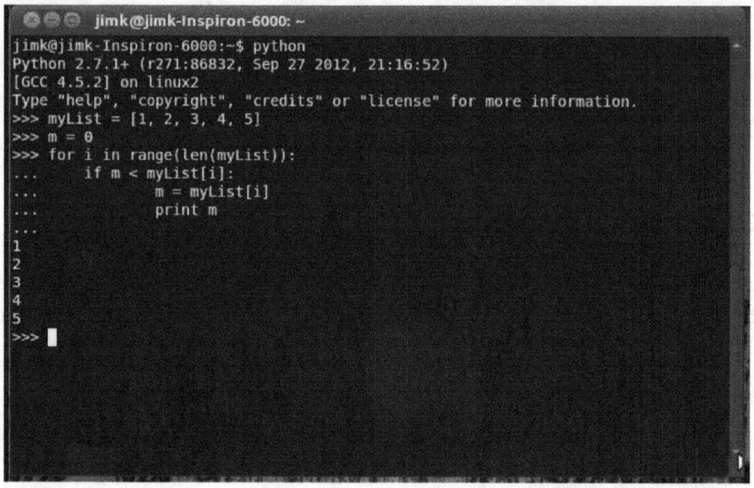

Figure 4.6.2

This program creates a list with values 1 through 5. Then uses a for loop to step through the list moving each element to a variable and then printing the contents of that variable.

List (array) containing both numbers and strings.

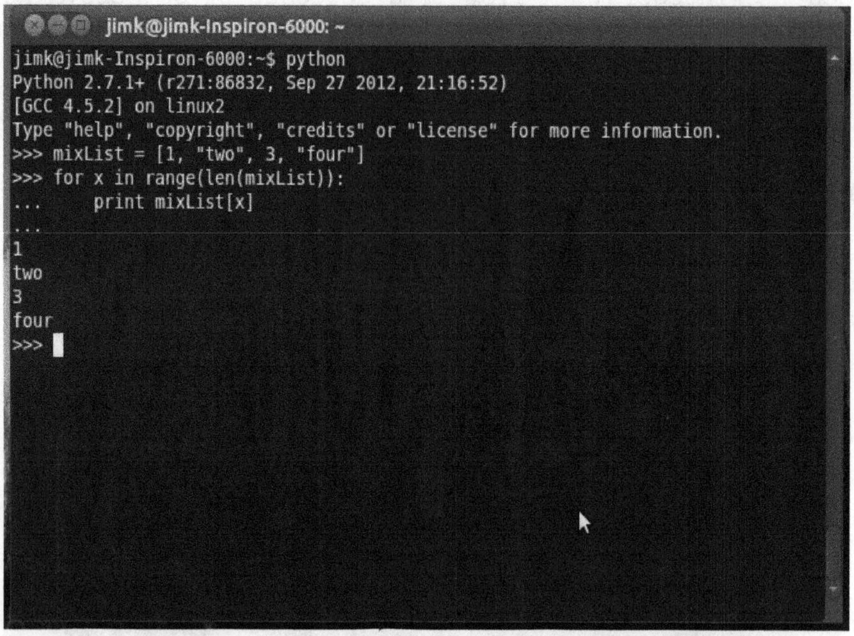

Figure 4.6.3

A Python list can contain mixed data types. A list containing both numbers and strings is created. Then uses a for loop to step through the list printing the contents of each element.

Append data to an empty list (array).

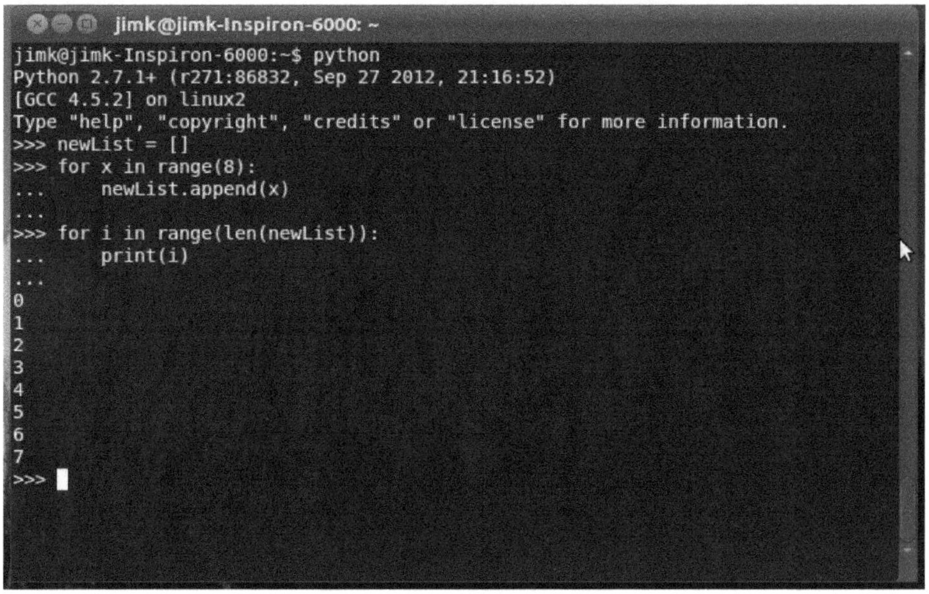

Figure 4.6.4

In most programming languages you can't assign a value to a list or array element that doesn't exist. However, you can append to a list in Python, making the list more flexible than the array found in most other programming languages. In this example, a null array (an array that does not have any initial values) is created. Then a for loop is used to add eight (8) values to the list. The second part of the program prints the values inserted into the list. Note the eight values printed are zero (0) through seven (7).

Two-Dimensional List (array).

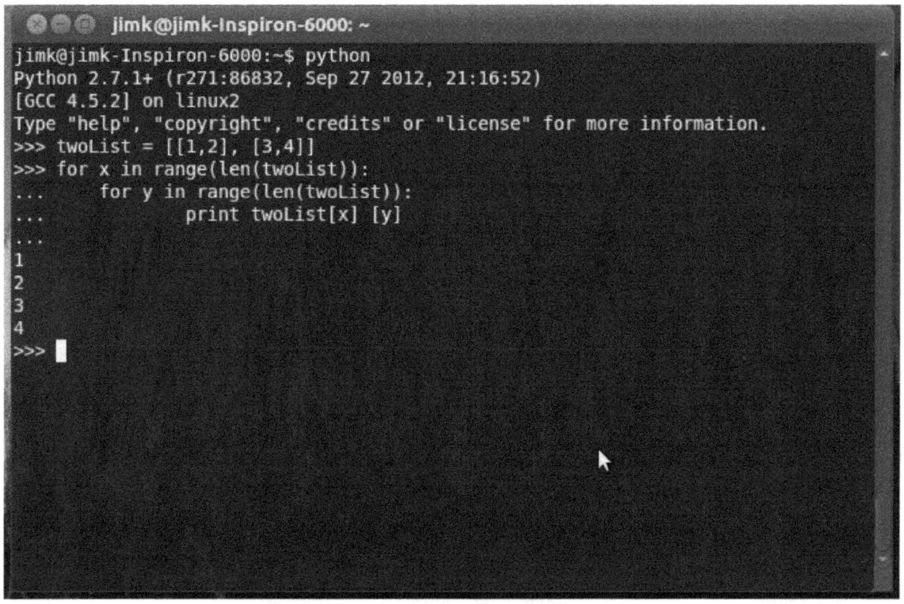

Figure 4.6.5

Python lists can also accommodate two-dimensional arrays. In the example the list defined has two elements in two rows. Then uses some nested for loops to print the values in each of the 4 elements.

4.7 Summary

This lesson covered the repetition or looping structure. This covers the while, for, continue, and break statements. The while loop is a general purpose loop that can work as a counter controlled loop or a condition controlled loop (i.e. a flag, a sentinel, or a condition evaluating to true). A for loop is a counter controlled loop used when a loop is to be executed a number of times.

Lists are Python's answer to arrays. Python lists are very flexible and offer features not generally available in other programming languages.

Lesson 4 - Quiz

1. The Repetition Structure may also be referred to as the:
a. Continue Structure
b. Decision Structure
c. Sequence Structure
d. Looping Structure

2. The _____ loop executes as long as the condition evaluates to TRUE.
a. while
b. range
c. continuous
d. decision

3. Only the first statement of a loop needs to be indented.
a. True
b. False

4. The for loop is known as a _____ loop.
a. boolean
b. range controlled
c. counter controlled
d. infinite

5. In Python, the for statement uses the _____ function to determine start value, end value and increment or decrement.
a. range()
b. increment()
c. decrement()
d. size()

6. Loops within loops are referred to as _____ loops.
a. repetition
b. nested
c. interior
d. infinite

7. The _____ command transfers control to the program statement immediately following the last statement in the loop.
a. continue
b. break
c. skip
d. goback

8. The _____ command transfers control back to the beginning of the loop.
a. continue
b. break
c. skip
d. goback

9. The range() function returns a list of _____.
a. random values
b. string values
c. consecutive integers
d. consecutive letters

10.   A Python List can contain mixed data types.
a. True
b. False

Lesson 4 - Exercises

Exercise 4.1 Sum Grades.

Enter the following code in the Python command line.

```
sum = 0
response = 0
while response != -999:
        sum = sum + response
        response = input("Enter grade or -999 to end: ")
```

    [hit the enter key twice]
    [enter values below, type the following line:]

```
        print "Sum of Grades: " + str(sum)
```

Test your program using:

```
        23
        44
        52
        65
        -999
```

RESULT: 183

Exercise 4.2 Average Rainfall

Enter the following code in the Python command line.

```
        sum = 0
        for count in range 1, 5):
            rain = input("Enter the weekly rainfall: ")
            sum = sum + rain


        avg = sum / 4
        print "Average rainfall: " + str(avg)
```

Test your program using:

```
        12
        .9
        4.3
        1.1
```

RESULT: 4.575

Exercise 4.3 Average Grade

Five tests are given in a semester. Write a program that will calculate the average of the grades for the five tests.

Test your program using:

    100
    87
    55
    91
    75

Exercise 4.4 Compute Deposit

Write a program that allows the user to enter the amounts of several checks (exact quantity unknown). Then the program should print out the sum of the value of the checks entered.

Test your program using:

    104.87
    97.50
    1234.56
    8.45

Lesson 5 - Python Script Files

Objectives:

- Create a Python script file.
- Execute a Python script file.
- List text editors for various operating systems.
- Use comments in your Python script file.

5.1 Python Script Files

Entering your program at the command line is not the best way to write your Python programs. You have to type them in each time you want to run them. The solution, Python script files. Using any text editor, type in your program then execute it through python.

Figure 5.1.1

5.2 Using Text Editors

Every version of Linux, Windows and MAC OS/X come with an installed text editor. On top of that there are numerous text editors available, many for free for each of these platforms. In addition, most word processors can produce text files.

Windows: Windows comes with Notepad installed. Notepad is sufficient for creating Python scripts. A better choice would be a free download called Notepad++. Once you get the hang of it and learn all the stuff it can do, this will be your choice.

Mac OS/X: comes with TextEdit installed. This is a primitive text editor, not good for much but entering text. The good news is that there are two free text editors for download called Smultron and TextWrangler. These are quality text editors with all the bells and whistles.

Linux: Ubuntu 15.10 loads Gedit by default. I use this for several examples in this chapter. It is a good text editor and many use it. It is a far cry from what linux users had in the past (and is still available), the basic text editor simply known as "vi". This cryptic hard to use and understand text editor is available on every Unix and Linux system and runs the same on each one, and that is the beauty of vi.

My personal favorite is from the KDE GUI collection, it is called Kate. It is, for me, the editor of choice mainly because I have used it for years and I am most

50

familiar with it. Other editors like Kedit, nano, vim, emacs, and many others are all adequate text editors.

5.3 Creating Python Script Files

The first line [#! /usr/bin/python] should be the first line of ALL your python programs. If you include this line, some versions of python on linux systems will allow you to do a chmod instruction to make it executable and then you do not have to run from the python environment.

The python script is just the commands we ran from the command line in a text file.

For example:

Figure 5.3.1

5.4 Decision Scripts

We have some examples of scripts using the decision structure. You can run these as scripts as they are, you ran the same instructions from the command line. These scripts were generated using the Kate text editor.

Figure 5.4.1

51

An example of a nested if structure.

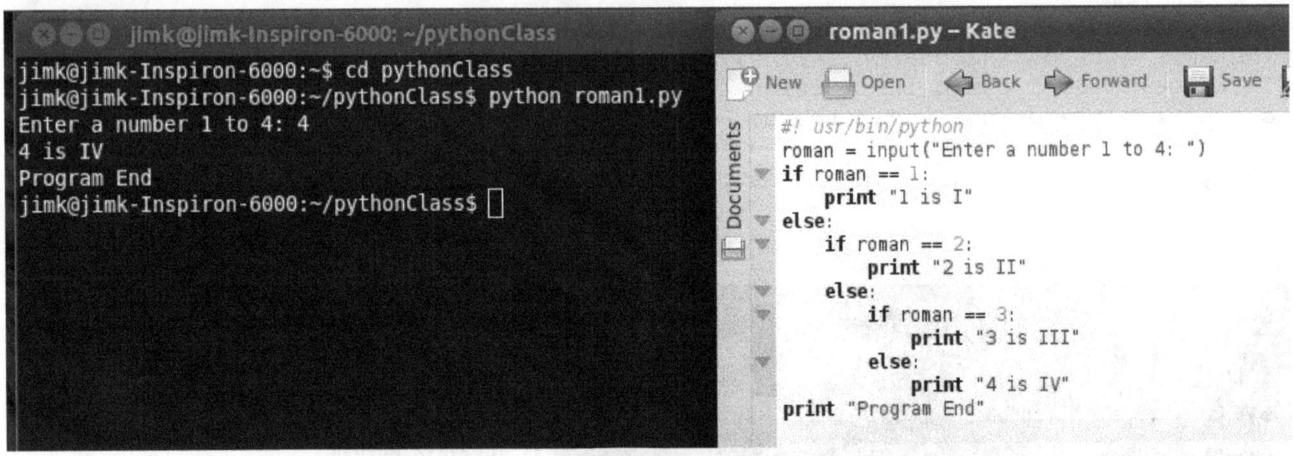

Figure 5.4.2

5.5 Repetition Scripts

Here are some of the same programs we ran from the command line to illustrate repetition.

Figure 5.5.1

The range of the for loop starts with a value of 120. It ends with a value of 10. This indicates a decrement loop and the decrement value is a negative 10 (-10). Each time through the loop the num variable is decremented by 10 until it reaches 10. Note the last value printed is 20. This is because when the variable num is decremented to 10 it is evaluated and the step to print the contents of num is skipped.

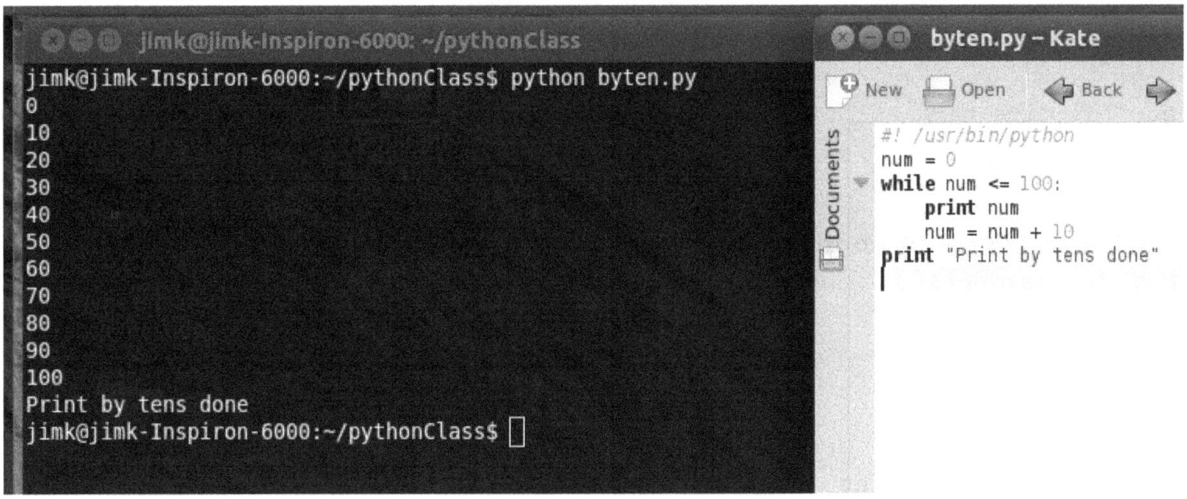

Figure 5.5.2

5.6 Comments

The sole purpose of comments is to provide inline documentation for your program. Having comments in a program helps the programmer to remember the purpose of some of the code as well as assist other programmers who may have to maintain or interpret the code. It is always a good idea to provide lots of comments in programs that will be used by others.

A comment is simply a line preceded by a #. The code below shows a comment for a for loop in a program.

```
# this loop counts to ten
for i in range(10):
print i
```

5.7 Executing Script Files

Python script files can always be executed from the Python environment. The first line of a Python program should be #! /usr/bin/python and the name should have an extension of .py.

Some linux versions will allow a chmod instruction on a Python file to make it executable from the command line without entering the Python environment.

The syntax for executing a Python script file:

```
$ python filename.py
```

Start the Python environment, then the name of the file containing the Python script. This file should have the .py extension.

5.8 Sample Program

In your favorite text editor, create a file named fme.py and enter the following code:

```
    #! /usr/bin/python
for i in range(10):
x = 0.1*i
print x
print x/(1-x*x)
```

Execute the program in the terminal window.

python fme.py

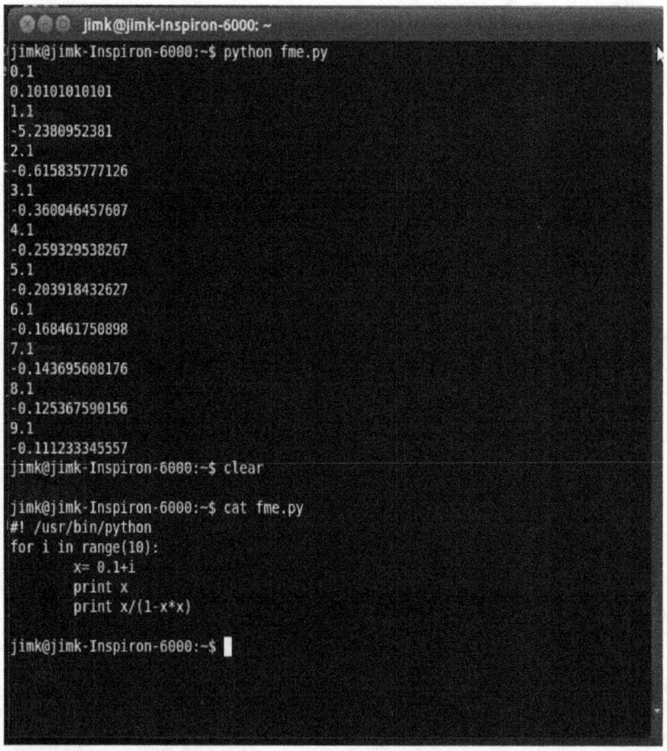

Figure 5.8.1

5.9 Summary

Python script files are files that can be called in the Python environment when they are needed. It allow the programmer to use his or her favorite text editor to generate the Python code, and store that code for use when it is required. Also, by using the text editor, scripts can be fixed, change, added to, whenever needed.

54

If the operating system is Unix or Linux, the chmod instruction can make the script file executable so it can be executed outside the Python environment.

Each Python script should have the first line:

#! /usr/bin/python

and the file name should have an extension of

.py

for example mypythonprog.py.

This is required to make it executable outside the Python environment.

Lesson 5 - Quiz

1. You can use most text editors to create Python script files.
a.   True
b.   False

2. The first line of a script file should be:
a.   !import python
b.   #! /usr/bin/python
c.   #! /python/usr
d.   print Python

3. _____ are considered inline program documentation.
a.   commands
b.   operands
c.   comments
d.   functions

4. The _____ symbol at the start of a line indicates a comment.
a.   ?
b.   !
c. $
d.   #

5. The syntax for executing a Python program named filename.py is:
a.   filename.py
b.   python.py
c.   python filename.py
d.   filename.py python

6. Python script files must have the ____ extension.
a.   .py
b.   .odt
c.   .txt
d.   .python

7. The installed text editor for windows is:
a.   Smultron
b.   Notepad++
c.   Kate
d.   Notepad

8. _____ is a text editor for Mac OS/X that can be downloaded for free.
a.   TextWrangler
b.   Notepad++
c.   vi
d.   Photoshop

Lesson 5 - Exercises

Exercise 5.1 Rainfall Program

Enter the following script in a text editor and name it **twonum.py**. Save your program in your home directory and run it using the command:

```
$ python twonum.py
```

```python
#! /usr/bin/python
num1 = input("Enter the first number: ")
num2 = input("Enter the second number: ")
sum = num1 + num2
print "The sum of the numbers is " + str(sum)
```

Exercise 5.2 Vote Program (decision)

Enter the following script in a text editor and name it **voteone.py**. Save your program in your home directory and run it using the command:

```
$ python voteone.py
```

```python
#! /usr/bin/python
age = input("Enter your age 0 to 100: ")
if age < 18:
    print "You may not vote"
else:
    print "You are allowed to vote"
```

Exercise 5.3 Repetition (For)

Enter the following script in a text editor and name it **wkrain.py**. Save your program in your home directory and run it using the command:

```
$ python wkrain.py
```

```python
#! /usr/bin/python
sum = 0
for count in range (1, 5):
    rain = input("Enter the weekly rainfall: ")
    sum = sum + rain
    avg = sum / 4
print "Average rainfall: " + str(avg)
```

Exercise 5.4 Vote Program (nested if)

Enter the following script in a text editor and name it **votetwo.py**. Save your program in your home directory and run it using the command:

```
$ python votetwo.py
```

```
#! /usr/bin/python
age = input("Enter your age 0 to 100: ")
registered = input("Enter 1 for registered or 2 for not registered: ")
if age < 18:
    print "You may not vote"
else:
    if registered = 1:
            print "You are allowed to vote"
    else:
            print "You must register to vote"
```

Exercise 5.5 On Your own

Write a Python program that will ask for the amount of a loan between $3000 and $100000. If the loan is less than $50000 the interest will be 10%. If the loan is greater than $50000 but less than $75000 the interest will be 9% and if the loan is over $75000 the interest is 8.25%. Calculate the interest for one year on the amount given and show the amount of the loan, the interest percentage and the total interest for the year. Also show the total of the amount of the loan plus the interest.

Lesson 6 - Python Functions and Modules

Objectives:

- Explain how to define a function.
- Differentiate Required Arguments, Keyword Arguments, and Default Arguments.
- Code a function call.
- Return data from a function.
- Describe the use of Python modules.

6.1 Overview of Python Functions

A function is a reusable set of code that will return a value when called by a program. Python has some internal functions to do common tasks like read a file, write a file, close a file, some common mathematical operations, file manipulation, etc.. This lesson will focus on functions that can be created by the programmer to do tasks that may be repeated in a program or group of programs. Write and test once and use many times is the value of using functions.

6.2 Defining a Function

Defining a function only names the function and specifies the arguments to be used by the function. It also contains the instructions that are to be executed by the function. The function should have a name that effectively communicates the purpose of the function. The name should not be too long but give some indication of the purpose of the function. This will help the programmers that use the function in debugging programs.

A function is a reusable set of code that will return a value when called by a program. The rules for defining a function are:

- Functions begin with the keyword **def** followed by the function name and a set of parenthesis ()
- Arguments (parameters) are placed within the parenthesis.
- The code block within every function begins with a colon (:) and must be indented.
- The first statement line of a function may be a comment line.
- The **return [expression]** statement is used to, optionally pass back an expression or value to the calling program.

SYNTAX:

```
def functionname( [arguments] ):
function statements
return [return value expression]
```

The keyword **def** is followed by the name of the function and then a set of parenthesis that will contain the arguments passed to the function if any are passed. It is not necessary for a function to have any arguments passed.

6.3 Arguments or Parameters

All arguments in the Python language are passed by reference. Any changes made in the function will be reflected back to the calling function. A functions arguments are passed in the sequence expected by the function. The number of arguments passed must match, exactly the sequence and number of arguments expected by the function definition. These arguments are called the "Required Arguments".

```
def showName( title ):
print title;
return;
# now the function
showName("Cats");
```

An argument in a function can be given a default value. If a value is not provided for an argument, the value set as a default would be passed to the function. This is known as a "Default Argument".

```
def showName( title, days=30 ):
print title;
print days;
return;
# now the function
showName("Cats");
```

Above is the code to print the show title and the default value. Below is the code that will print the show title and 15 as the number of days.

```
def showName( title, days=30 ):
print title;
print days;
return;
# now the function
showName("Cats", 15);
```

6.4 Sample Function

Now we will code the solution to a problem using Python.

PROBLEM: Four friends go to dinner in Ocean City, Maryland. The bill is presented after dinner in the following amounts: Dave's dinner is $27; Bobbies dinner is $20; Joan's dinner is $24; and Jim's dinner is $22. They are taking advantage of a winter special coupon offering 10% off the entire check (Before Tax). The tax in Ocean City is 5% and the typical expected dinner gratuity is 20%. Calculate the total bill. The tip is calculated before tax. At the end the bill will be split evenly between the two couples.

Using your favorite editor, create the following script:

```
#!/usr/bin/python
# The four functions we will use in calculations.
def add4(a, b, c, d);
 print "SUM %d + %d + %d + %d" % (a, b, c, d)
    return a + b + c + d
def sub(a, b);
    print "SUB %d - %d" % (a, b)
    return a - b
def mul(a, b);
    print "MUL %d * %d" % (a, b)
    return a * b
def div(a, b);
    print "SUM %d / %d" % (a, b)
     return a / b

# Use the functions to calculate the bill and split.
dinners = add4(23, 24, 27, 20)
discount = sub(dinners, 1.10)
tip = mul(dinner, .20)
tax = mul(dinner, .05)
total = add4(discount, tip, tax, 0)
split = div(total, 2)

# Display Results
print "Dinner: %d" % (dinner)
print "Dinner less 10 percent: %d" % (discount)
print "Tax: %d" % (tax)
print "Tip: %d" % (tip)
print "Total Bill: %d" % (total)
print "Per Couple: %d" % (split)
```

The above example has three sections. The first section defines four functions.
The first function adds four values. The second function subtracts the second
value from the first value. The third function multiplies the first value by the
second value. The fourth function divides the first value by the second value.
The second section uses the functions for calculation of the problem. Note the
statement calculating the "total". There are only three values needed for the
calculation, so we send a 0 for the fourth value which does not affect the final
value. The third section displays the calculated values.

6.5 Modules

A Python module is a tool for organizing your code. Keeping related code in a
module structure, makes your code easier to use an understand. A module may
contain functions, classes, executable code and variables. There are built-in
modules standard in python and user defined modules which are created by the user.
We will look at some built-in modules in the next chapter. This lesson will focus
on user defined modules.

61

Any Python source file may be used as a module, simply by importing the code into another program using the "import" command.

```
import module1 [, module 2 [, .... moduleN]]
```

A module is loaded only once and it may then be used as many times as needed.

6.6 Sample Module

PROBLEM: Create two modules. The first module will calculate Celsius to Fahrenheit and the second module will calculate Fahrenheit to Celsius. Then create a demo program to test the modules that imports and uses both modules.

Name the Celsius to Fahrenheit module c2f.py and the Fahrenheit to Celsius module f2c.py. Name the test program temptest.py. Store all three programs in the same directory.

c2f.py

```
#!/usr/bin/python
# Calculate Celsius to Fahrenheit
def celfah(a);
     celsius = (a - 32) * 5 / 9
     print "CELSIUS: %d FAHRENHEIT: %d" % (celsius, a)
return
```

f2c.py

```
#!/usr/bin/python
# Calculate Fahrenheit to Celsius
def fahcel(a);
     fahrenheit = (a * 9 / 5) + 32
     print "FAHRENHEIT: %d CELSIUS: %d" % (fahrenheit, a)
return
```

Then create the program to test the two modules.

temptest.py

```
#!/usr/bin/python
# Use the c2f.py and the f2c.py modules
# Import the Modules
import c2f.py
import f2c.py
# Now we can use the modules to print results
print "Test Conversions"
c2f.celfah(0)
c2f.celfah(100)
```

62

```
f2c.fahcel(32)
f2c.fahcel(212)
print "End of Program temptest.py"
```

The program simply passes a temperature value to one of the modules. The modules
do the calculation and print the calculated value plus the original value.

6.7 Summary

A function is a reusable set of code that will return a value when called by a
program. Python has some internal functions to do common tasks like read a file,
write a file, close a file, some common mathematical operations, file manipulation,
etc.. This lesson will focus on functions that can be created by the programmer to
do tasks that may be repeated in a program or group of programs. Write and test
once and use many times is the value of using functions.

A Python module is a tool for organizing your code. Keeping related code in a
module structure, makes your code easier to use an understand. A module may
contain functions, classes, executable code and variables. There are built-in
modules standard in python and user defined modules which are created by the user.
We will look at some built-in modules in the next chapter. This lesson will focus
on user defined modules.

Lesson 6 - Quiz

1. A _____ is a reusable set of code that will return a value when called by a program.
a. module
b. function
c. block
d. schema

2. Functions begin with a keyword _____.
a. def
b. func
c. mod
d. arg

3. Function arguments are placed before the parenthesis.
a. True
b. False

4. All arguments in the Python language are passed by _____.
a. keyword
b. value
c. indicator
d. reference

5. An argument in a function can be given a default value.
a. True
b. False

6. A Python _____ is a tool for organizing your code.
a. block
b. schema
c. module
d. class

7. A module may contain:
a. functions
b. classes
c. variables
d. all of the above

8. A module is loaded every time it is needed by the program.
a. True
b. False

9. There are _____ modules that are standard in Python.
a. built-in
b. user defined
c. class
d. block

10. Modules created by the user are referred to as _____ modules.
a. built-in
b. user defined
c. class
d. block

Lesson 6 - Exercises

Exercise 6.1 Temperature Conversion

Write a Python program that will print a table of Celsius temperatures and the Fahrenheit equivalents between 0 and 100 Celsius. The program should print temperatures in 10 degree increments. The program must have a function named celsius2fahrenheit. This function should receive a Celsius temperature convert it to Fahrenheit and return the result to the calling program.

The formula for conversion is:

Fahrenheit = 9.0 / 5.0 * Celsius + 32

Get the program working on your computer. Then, study and understand the solution below. It should help you do the other exercises in this chapter.

```
def celsius2fahrenheit(celsius):
    """This function converts a Celsius temp ***
    fahrenheit = 9.0/5.0 * celsius + 32
    return fahrenheit
for celsius in range(0, 101, 10):
    print celsius, "\t", celsius2fahrenheit(celsius)
```

Exercise 6.2 Interest

Write a Python program that will calculate the interest for one year on a loan at five (5) different interest rates: (3%, 3.5%, 4%, 4.5%, 5%). The program should display the five different interest results. The function should receive the interest percentage from the calling program and return the interest value. The function should be named calc_int.

The interest formula is:

Interest = Amount of Loan * Interest Rate * Term of Loan

Exercise 6.3 Fence

Write a Python program that will calculate the number of feet and cost of wire required to fence in a farmer's field. The fence costs $.82 per foot for each strand of wire. The farmer intends to string three strands of wire completely around his field. The program should ask the user for the length and width of the field. It should include a function that takes the total number of feet required and calculate the total cost of the wire. Name the function cost_wire.

Lesson 7 - Files

Objectives:
- Describe methods and modes for opening files.
- Use the close() method for files.
- Explain how to write text files.
- Explain how to read text files.
- Use the tell() and seek() methods to position file cursor.

7.1 Overview of Python Files

Python has a rich set of methods to support using files. There are methods to create, manipulate and delete files. Python can operate on both text and binary files. It also has methods to rename files, delete files as well as create and delete directories.

7.2 Open and Close Files

Before a file can be read or written, it must be opened. The program needs to be able to find the file (if it exists) or open the file if it has not been created. Then it needs to state how the file will be used, input, output or both. Should existing data be overwritten or appended to. Expect text or binary data. This information is all gathered at the open() method. The syntax for this method is:

fileobject = open(filename [, accessmode] [, buffering])

The fileobject name will be used to identify the file. The file name in the open method is the name of the file to be used or created. The accessmode is how the file will allow the data to be accessed. The buffering will contain bufffering information.

Accessmode	result
r	read
rb	Read binary mode
r+	Read and write
rb+	Read and write binary mode
w	Write binary
w+	Read and write
wb+	Read and write binary files
a	Append to existing file
ab	Append to existing binary file
a+	Append to a file and read the file
ab+	Append and read to a binary file

66

Buffering	result
0	No buffering
1	Line buffering
>1	Indicated buffer size
<0 (negative)	System default buffer size

Once opened with a fileobject name there are several commands that will assist the program with some information about the file opened.

Command	Result
Fileobject.closed	Set to true if closed
Fileobject.name	Returns the name of the file
Fileobject.mode	Returns the access mode of the file
Fileobject.softspace	Returns false if space explicitly required with print otherwise true

```python
#!/usr/bin/python
myfile = open("mytext.txt", "r+")
print "Name of file   : ", myfile.name
print "Opening mode   : ", myfile.mode
print "Closed or not : ", myfile.closed
print "Softspace flag: ", myfile.softspace
```

The close() method flushes the buffer and closes the file so no further action can be taken on the file until it is reopened.

```python
fileobject.close()
myfile.close()
```

```python
#!/usr/bin/python
myfile = open("mytext.txt", "r+")
print "Name of file   : ", myfile.name
print "Opening mode   : ", myfile.mode
print "Closed or not : ", myfile.closed
print "Softspace flag: ", myfile.softspace
myfile.close()
```

7.3 Writing Files

Python writes data to files and extend existing files by opening the file in append mode. It should be noted than the write method does not add a newline ("\n") to the end of a string.

```
fileobject.write(sring)<br />
myfile.write("Hello, World\n")
```

```
#!/usr/bin/python
myfile = open("mytext.txt", "w+")
myfile.write("This is a Python output file\nI will read it in the
next       exercise.\n")
myfile.close()
```

7.4 Reading Files

Once a file is opened and it exists, it can be read by the program. Either for purposes of processing or printing. There are three (3) read methods:
```
read()
readline()
readlines()
```
The read() method can read a specified number of bytes or read the entire file. If the file contains:
```
                DarthVader
```
The following reads:
```
            method1=myfile.read(1)
            method2=myfile.read()
```
Will return:
```
            method1 = D
            method2 = arthVader
```

A pointer is returned that shows were each read ends. To examine the contents of this pointer use the tell() method:

```
        print myfile.tell()
```

The readline() method reads an entire line or until the number of bytes specified has been reached.

The readlines() reads lines until the end of file is recognized or the number of bytes specified has been reached.

```
        print myfile.readlines()
```

There are many ways to use the read instructions. However, in programming, the programmer should be consistent in using various instructions and methods.

7.5 A Program Using Files

Read and print the entire file.

```python
#!/usr/bin/python
myfile = open("mytext.txt", "r")
print myfile.read()
myfile.close()
```

Read and print the first 16 characters of a file.

```python
#!/usr/bin/python
myfile = open("mytext.txt", "r")
print myfile.read(16)
myfile.close()
```

Read and print the first line of a file.

```python
#!/usr/bin/python
myfile = open("mytext.txt", "r")
print myfile.readline()
myfile.close()
```

Read and print all lines of a file.

```python
#!/usr/bin/python
myfile = open("mytext.txt", "r")
print myfile.readlines()
myfile.close()
```

Read and print the entire file alternative method.

```python
#!/usr/bin/python
myfile = open("mytext.txt", "r")
for line in myfile:
        print line,
myfile.close()
```

7.6 Summary

The ability to save data to external files and use them as input to other programs is a vital function of most programming languages. Python has a very powerful and flexible suite of functions that allow the program to read, write and maintain files.

Lesson 7 - Quiz

1. Python has a set of methods to:
a. create files
b. manipulate files
c. delete files
d. all of the above

2. Before a file can be used it must be _____.
a. examined
b. opened
c. appended
d. recognized

3. Adding data to the end of a file is to _____ data to the file.
a. concatenate
b. append
c. extend
d. none of the above

4. The _____ is the parameter in the open method that tells how the file will be accessed.
a. accessmode
b. append
c. openmode
d. readmode

5. The _____ method flushes the write buffer.
a. flush()
b. close()
c. end()
d. quit()

6. The write method adds a newline ("\n") to the end of a string.
a. True
b. False

7. Which is NOT a read method.
a. read()
b. readline()
c. readlines()
d. readfile()

8. To examine the contents of the read pointer, use the _____ method.
a. count()
b. pointer()
c. tell()
d. show()

9. Whic command reads the entire file named myfile into a variable named method2.
a. method2 = myfile.read(all)
b. method2 = myfile.read()
c. method2 = myfile.read(1)
d. method2 = myfile.read(n)

10.   Python can operate only on text files.
a. True
b. False

Lesson 7 - Exercises

Exercise 7.1 Enter your user name

Enter the following code in the Python command line.

```
uname = raw_input("Enter your user name: ")
if uname != "Sam":
    print "ACCESS DENIED!"
```

Test your program using:

```
ann
sam
Sam
```

Exercise 7.2 Pass or Fail

Enter the following code in the Python command line.

```
grade = input("Enter your grade 0 to 100: ")
if grade < 60:
    print "You did not pass"
else:
    print "You passed"
```

Test your program using:

```
55
97
60
```

Exercise 7.3 Nested If

Enter the following code in the Python command line.

```
balance = input("Enter your bank account balance: ")
if balance < 100:
    print "You will not get any interest"
else:
    if balance >= 100:
    print "You will receive five percent interest"
```

Test your program using:

```
100
97.50
1234.56
```

Exercise 7.4 On your own

Using what you have learned, write a Python program that asks the user for a magazine name and if they want a six month or a twelve month subscription. A six month subscription costs $8.49 and a twelve month subscription costs $14.99. The program should print out the name of the magazine and the cost for the subscription length selected.

Lesson 8 - Tkinter

Objectives:

- Introduce Tkinter and Tk.
- Use basic Tkinter commands
- Place widgets using Pack Manager
- Place widgets using Grid Manager
- Use basic Tkinter widgets.
- Create windows using Tkinter widgets.

8.1 Overview of Tkinter

Python offers various graphical user interfaces (GUI). Tkinter is the interface to the Tk toolkit that is included in Python. The Tk toolkit is a set of graphics tools for creating window user interfaces. The Tk toolkit is a popular GUI toolkit found in most Linux distributions as part of the Tcl language. The name Tkinter is the combination of Tk + interface. Together, Tkinter and Python are able to create GUI applications quickly and easily.

To determine if Tkinter is installed on your computer, open a terminal window and at the command prompt type: **python**

Enter:
>>>**import Tkinter**
>>>**Tkinter._test()**

That should result in a screen like this:

The steps required to create GUI applications involve the following steps:
- Import Tkinter
- Create the application main window
- Add widgets
- Enter the main event loop that will perform actions based on events triggered by the user.

CODE EXAMPLE:

```
import Tkinter
x=Tkinter.Tk()
x.mainloop()
```

This should produce the following window:

Tkinter widgets (or controls) are used in GUI applications. In this lesson we will look at some of the basic widgets that are commonly used.

Label	Button	Entry	Text	SpinBox	ListBox
Canvas	Menu	CheckButton		RadioButton	

There are other Tkinter widgets but they are beyond the scope of this lesson.

The following lessons describe the basic widgets in a simple example designed to show the basic use of the widget. I have designed a template (template.py) that I use for the basis of all these examples. This is to standardize the structure and simplify the explanation.

template.py

```
#!/usr/bin/python
from Tkinter import *
import Tkinter

home = Tk()
home.geometry("200x200")
home.title("Template")

# widgets here

mainloop()
```

This code does the following:
1. **from Tkinter import *** and **import Tkinter** – these lines are redundant. I included both because some use one and some use the other. I prefer to use the **from Tkinter import ***
2. **home = Tk()** – Establishes the root or main or master window. I name the root window **home** for consistency in my examples.
3. **home.geometry("200x200")** – this line establishes the size of the window created in pixels. If this is omitted a window just large enough to hold the widgets will be created. I used 200 wide (first 200) and 200 high (second 200) as a basic window. As you will note I change sizes according to how the window is used in an example.
4. **home.title("Template")** – If this line is not included the top bar of the window will say Tk. I like to title my windows with a meaningful title.
5. **# widgets here** – This is a comment line. In most examples, this is where I place the code to place a widget on the window. Comment lines have no effect on the running of the program. They exist solely as documentation for the programmer.
6. **mainloop()** – this is the command that displays the window.

You will find all of these commands in each of the examples. Please feel free to make changes, this is how you learn. I make available all of the code on my web site so you don't even have to type a line. However, I caution you that this is NOT the way to learn Python programming. Enter the code, make changes to the code and see what happens. If you screw up the code you can always get another copy. I would encourage you to work with copies of my code and always have an original to go back to if you mess up. By experimentation with the code you will learn. Do research on the widgets on the internet. There are many different ways to use the widgets and other methods and attributes that I do not explain in my simple overview.

The code for this template plus the code for all of the examples are available on the author's web site. These were all developed and tested on Mac OS/X but should work on all other platforms.

You can run template.py and it should look like this:

8.2 Pack and Grid Managers

There are two ways to place widgets on the window, the Pack Manager and the Grid Manager. When developing your window it is advisable to pick one manager and stick with it and don't try to mix managers on the same window.

The Pack manager format is:

widget.pack()

This packs the widget to the parent window and places it in a best fit location. It may be centered or may be left justified.

<u>pack.py</u>
```
#!/usr/bin/python
from Tkinter import *
import Tkinter

home = Tk()
home.geometry("200x200")
home.title("Template")

b1 = Button(home, text="Submit")
b2 = Button(home, text="Cancel")
b1.pack()
b2.pack()

mainloop()
```

This should produce two buttons that look like this:

The Grid Manager places the widgets in cells in a grid (or table). This gives the programmer more control on where a widget is placed. A widget may be put in a single cell on a single row in a single column or the rows and columns may be joined together to allow for a larger area to store a widget.

The Grid Manager format is:

> **widget.grid([grid_options)**

Now build the same two buttons as used in pack but use the grid manager.

<u>grid.py</u>

```
#!/usr/bin/python
from Tkinter import *
import Tkinter

home = Tk()
home.geometry("200x200")
home.title("Template")

b1 = Button(home, text="Submit")
b2 = Button(home, text="Cancel")
b1.grid(row=0, column=0)
b2.grid(row=1, column=1)

mainloop()
```

Now note the placement of the buttons as compared to the placement of the buttons using pack.

8.3 Label

The first widget we will explore is the Label widget. This is usually used to, as its name implies, label another control or controls. You can also use it to display a .gif image as we will see in a future lesson. Labels are most often used in conjuction with the Entry widget.

<u>label.py</u>

```
#!/usr/bin/python
from Tkinter import *
import Tkinter

home = Tk()
home.geometry("250x75")
home.title("Demo Label Widget")

lab = Label(home, text="Demo Label Widget")
lab.pack()

mainloop()
```

You already know the commands for the widgets surrounding the two lines that start with the name **lab**

1. **lab = Label(home, text="Demo Label Widget")**
    1. lab - a variable name to identify the Label widget
    2. Label - instruction to create a label widget.
    3. home - identifies the window where the widget will be placed.
    4. text="Demo Label Widget" - text to appear on the label. (Feel free to change anything between the double quotes.
2. **lab.pack()** - this instruction uses the pack() method to place the command stored in the variable lab on the window designated in the command. If you don't include this command your label will not show on the window.

8.4 Button

Buttons are used to trigger events. This example simply shows how to create a button on the window. Later examples will show how to create events that will happen when the button is clicked.

<u>button.py</u>

```
#!/usr/bin/python
from Tkinter import *
import Tkinter
```

```
home = Tk()
home.geometry("100x100")
home.title("Demo Button Widget")

btn = Button(home, text="GET")
btn.pack()
mainloop()
```

The two lines that create the GET button:
1. **btn = Button(home, text="GET")**
    1. btn - a variable name to identify the Button widget
    2. Button - instruction to create a button widget.
    3. home - identifies the window where the widget will be placed.
    4. text="GET" - text to appear on the button. (Feel free to change anything between the double quotes.
2. **btn.pack()** - this instruction uses the pack() method to place the command stored in the variable btn on the window designated in the command. If you don't include this command your button will not show on the window.

8.5 Entry

The entry widget accepts user input. As was noted in the Label lesson, I have included a label as well as the entry widget. The label is there to tell the user what is the expected entry into the Entry widget.

<u>entry.py</u>

```
#!/usr/bin/python
from Tkinter import *
import Tkinter

home = Tk()
home.geometry("300x100")
home.title("Demo Label & Entry Widgets")

lab = Label(home,text="User: ")
lab.pack()

inp = Entry(home)
inp.pack()

mainloop()
```

The two lines that begin with lab are explained in the Lesson for the Label widget.
The two lines that begin with inp create and display the Entry widget

1. **inp = Entry(home)**
    1. inp - a variable name to identify the Entry widget.
    2. Entry - instruction to create a data entry widget.
    3. home - identifies the window where the widget will be placed.
2. **inp.pack()** - this instruction uses the pack() method to place the command stored in the variable inp on the window designated in the command. If you don't include this command your data entry widget will not show on the window.

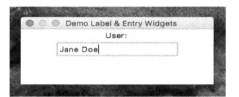

8.6 Text

The Text widget is used to display multiple lines of text on the window. An example might be a window that gives the user instructions to complete a task.

<u>text.py</u>

```
#!/usr/bin/python
from Tkinter import *
import Tkinter

home = Tk()
home.geometry("200x75")
home.title("Demo Text Widget")

txt = Text(home, height=3, width=30)
txt.pack()

msg = "Your instructions are to read this code carefully and
understand it."
txt.insert(END, msg)

mainloop()
```

There are four lines that are needed to put out the text widget. The first two lines put the text box on the window. The last two create the message and place it in the text box.

1. **txt = Text(home, height=3, width=30)**
    1. txt is a variable name to hold the Text Widget instruction.
    2. Text is the widget name.
    3. home is the name of the window in which the text box will be placed.
    4. height=3 is the number of rows of text accomodated by the window.
    5. width=30 is the number of characters in the width of the window.
2. **txt.pack()**

3. **msg = "Your instructions ….and understand it"** - the message is stored in a variable called msg
4. **txt.insert(END, msg)** - The insert method is used to place the message in the text box.
    1. END places the text at the end of the contents of the text box. There are other options available.
    2. msg is the variable name that contains the message.

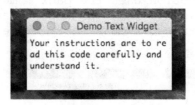

8.7 SpinBox

The SpinBox is used when the user needs to select from a range of numbers. While it is possible to use an Entry widget, the SpinBox only allows for a defined range of numbers for the user to make a selection. This can eliminate data entry errors and program processing problems with illegal values.

<u>spin.py</u>

```
#!/usr/bin/python
from Tkinter import *
import Tkinter

home = Tk()
home.geometry("250x75")
home.title("Demo Spinbox Widget")

spn = Spinbox(home, from_=0, to=10)
spn.pack()

mainloop()
```

The two lines that begin with spn are interpreted as follows:

1. **spn = Spinbox(home, from_=0, to=10)**
    1. spn – a variable name to identify the SpinBox widget.
    2. Spinbox – instruction to create a SpinBox widget.
    3. home – identifies the window where the widget will be placed.
    4. from_=0 – specifies zero (0) as the first value in the range.
    5. to=10 – specifies ten (10) as the last value in the range.
2. **spn.pack()** - this instruction uses the pack() method to place the command stored in the variable spn on the window designated in the command. If you don't include this command your SpinBox widget will not show on the window.

8.8 ListBox

A ListBox widget gives the user a list to select from. This is a fixed number of selections defined at programming time. When an item is selected from a list the number supplied with that item is stored for processing.

lbox.py

```
#!/usr/bin/python
from Tkinter import *
import Tkinter

home = Tk()
home.geometry("200x100")
home.title("Demo Listbox Widget")

lbx = Listbox(home)
lbx.pack()
lbx.insert(1, "Vanilla")
lbx.insert(2, "Chocolate")
lbx.insert(3, "Strawberry")
lbx.insert(4, "Rum Rasin")

mainloop()
```

In this example there are six lines associated with the ListBox widget:

1. **lbx = Listbox(home)**
   1. lbx – a variable name to identify the ListBox widget.
   2. Listbox – instruction to create a ListBox widget.
   3. home – identifies the window where the widget will be placed.
2. **lbx.pack()** - this instruction uses the pack() method to place the command stored in the variable lbx on the window designated in the command. If you don't include this command your ListBox widget will not show on the window.
3. **lbx.insert(#, "String value")** - the last four lines use the .insert method for a ListBox. Each line puts a String in the ListBox. The number that preceeds the string is the value that is passed to the program for processing.

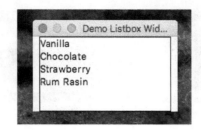

8.9 Image Using the Label Widget

The Label widget can be used for more than just a label. It can also display an image. NOTE that it supports .gif and not the more popular .png or .jpg. So to make this work you will need a .gif file. If you download the material from the author's web site you will get the logo.gif used in this example.

photo.py

```python
#!/usr/bin/python
from Tkinter import *
import Tkinter

master = Tk()
master.geometry("500x300")
master.title("Demo Label/Photo Widget")

photo = PhotoImage(file="logo.gif")
x = Label(master, image=photo)
x.photo = photo
x.pack()

mainloop()
```

There are four (4) lines associated with the inclusion of this widget.

1. **Photo = PhotoImage(file="logo.gif")**
   1. Photo – a variable name to identify the PhotoImage method.
   2. PhotoImage – a method to accept the location and name of image (.gif only).
   3. file="logo.gif" - location and name of .gif file to be used.
2. **x = Label(master, image=photo)**
   1. x – a variable name to identify the Label widget.
   2. Label – instruction to create a label widget.
   3. home – identifies the window where the widget will be placed.
   4. image=photo – tells the label widget to get an image from the photo variable.
3. **x.photo = photo**
   1. assigns the label variable to the photo method of the Label widget.
4. **x.pack()** - this instruction uses the pack() method to place the command stored in the variable x on the window designated in the command. If you don't include this command your label widget will not show on the window.

8.10 Canvas

The canvas widget allows the programmer to create graphics on the screen. Lines, Ellipses, Rectangles, Polygons and other graphics may be created. It is also possible to set up the canvas for the user to draw from the mouse. For the example we will draw an half circle (arc).

<u>canvas.py</u>

```python
#!/usr/bin/python
from Tkinter import *
import Tkinter

home = Tk()
home.geometry("300x300")
home.title("Demo Canvas Widget")

cnv = Tkinter.Canvas(home, bg="green", height=300, width=300)

point = 50, 50, 240, 210
arc = cnv.create_arc(point, start=0, extent=180, fill="yellow")

cnv.pack()
mainloop()
```

1. cnv = Tkinter.Canvas(home, bg="green", height=300, width=300)
    1. cnv – a variable name to identify the Canvas widget.
    2. Tkinter.Canvas – instruction to create a Canvas widget.
    3. home – identifies the window where the widget will be placed.
    4. bg="green" - the color of the background of the canvas.
    5. height=300 – the height of the canvas on the window.
    6. width=300 – the width of the canvas on the window.
2. point = 50, 50, 240, 210
    1. point – stores the starting point on the canvas and the ending point on the canvas. The x and y coordinates are shown for each.
3. arc = cnv.create_arc(point, start=0, extent=180, fill="yellow")
    1. arc – the variable that stores the variable containing the x,y coordinates for the starting and ending points, starting point on the canvas, the

degrees for the arc and the fill color for the arc.
4. cnv.pack() - this instruction uses the pack() method to place the command stored in the variable cnv on the window designated in the command. If you don't include this command your canvas widget will not show on the window.

There are several other simple shapes you can generate using similar code.

create_line(x, y, x1, y1, fill="#ffffff")
x is the x coordinate for the start of the line
y is the y coordinate for the start of the line
x1 is the x coordinate for the end of the line
y1 is the y coordinage for the end of the line
fill="#ffffff" is the hex value for the RGB color to be used.

create_rectangle(x, y, x1, y1, fill="#ffffff")
x is the x coordinate for the upper left corner of the rectangle
y is the y coordinate for the upper left corner of the rectangle
x1 is the x coordinate for the lower right corner of the rectangle
y1 is the y coordinate for the lower right corner of the rectangle
fill="#ffffff" is the hex value for the RGB color to be used.

create_oval(x, y, x1, y1, fill="#ffffff")
The coordinates are the same as listed for the rectangle. Tkinter draws an oval by creating a rectangle and inserting the oval within the rectangle. To create a circle, generate a rectangle with four equal sides.

create_polygon(x0, y0, x1, y1,... xn, yn, fill="#ffffff")
You need to supply x and y coordinates for each corner on the rectangle.

You may also use the canvas widget to display your pictures. The code to display a picture is illustrated below.

```python
#!/usr/bin/python
from Tkinter import *
import Tkinter

home = Tk()
home.geometry("400x400")
home.title("Template")

cnv = Tkinter.Canvas(home, bg="green", height=300, width=300)
cnv.pack()
img=PhotoImage(file="logo.gif")
```

```
cnv.create_image(20, 20, anchor="nw", image=img)

mainloop()
```

The same picture as was used in the label widget demo can be used for this demo.

8.11 Menu

Nearly every window we open on our computers has a menubar across the top. It usually goes something like this: File Edit View.......Help and the selections vary by applications. Using the Menu widget a similar menu may be constructed. The example in menu.py creates a menu item called languages which features five selections in its pull down menu.

<u>menu.py</u>

```
#!/usr/bin/python
from Tkinter import *
import Tkinter

home = Tk()
home.geometry("700x300")
home.title("Demo Menu Widget")

# Insert a menu bar on the main window
menubar = Menu(home)
home.config(menu=menubar)

# Create a menu button labeled "Language" that brings up a menu
# of four different Programming Languages
filemenu = Menu(menubar)
menubar.add_cascade(label='Language', menu=filemenu)

# Create five entries in the "Language" menu
# each command prints the name of the programming
# language selected.
def goPy(  ): print 'Python'
def goPHP(  ): print 'PHP'
def goCPP(  ): print 'C++'
def goVB(  ): print 'VB.NET'
filemenu.add_command(label='Python', command=goPy)
filemenu.add_command(label='PHP', command=goPHP)
filemenu.add_command(label='C++', command=goCPP)
filemenu.add_command(label='VB.NET', command=goVB)
filemenu.add_separator(  )
filemenu.add_command(label='Quit', command=sys.exit)

mainloop()
```

1. **menubar = Menu(home)** – first create a variable named menubar using the Menu widget and specify the name of the main window(in this case home)
2. **home.config(menu=menubar)** – use the config method of the home window to pass the contents to the menu attribute to the config method.
3. **filemenu = Menu(home)** – create a variable named filemenu with the Menu widget command Menu with the attribute home(the name of the root window).
4. **menubar.add_cascade(label='Language', menu=filemenu)** – the add_cascade() menthod builds the drop down menu.
   1. label='Language' - specifies that the visible title of the menu on the menubar will be Language.
   2. menu=filemenu - specifies the menu that will be used.
5. **def goXX(): print 'xxxxxx'** – a series of functions that are used by the add_command() method to print out a word indicating the Language selected. If a program was required to process the selection, this is where the program would be placed. In our example there are one for each selection except Quit which will be handled differently.
6. **filemenu.add_command(label='xxxxxx', command=goXX)** – the add_command() method reqires two attributes to create a menu selection.
   1. label='xxxxxx' - the name of the selection to add.
   2. command=goXX - the name of the function that processes the selection.
7. **filemenu.add_separator()** - puts a separator bar on the menu between selections.
8. **filemenu.add_command(label='Quit', command=sys.exit)** – This command will generate a Quit selection that will exit the window.

8.12 CheckButton

The CheckButton widget places a checkbutton on the window. A checkbutton is used when there are several possible selections and the user may select as many selections as needed. In our example the user is allowed to check as many operating systems in the list as they care to check.

<u>chkbtn.py</u>

```
#!/usr/bin/python
from Tkinter import *
import Tkinter

home = Tk()
```

```
home.geometry("200x200")
home.title("Demo Checkbutton Widget")

mb=  Menubutton (home, text="Operating Systems", relief=RAISED )
mb.grid()
mb.menu  =  Menu (mb, tearoff = 0 )
mb["menu"]  =  mb.menu

macVar  = IntVar()
ubuVar = IntVar()
winVar = IntVar()

mb.menu.add_checkbutton ( label="MAC OS/X",
                          variable=macVar )
mb.menu.add_checkbutton ( label="Ubuntu",
                          variable=ubuVar )
mb.menu.add_checkbutton ( label="Windows",
                          variable=winVar )

mb.pack()
mainloop()
```

1. **mb = Menubutton(home, text="Operating Systems", relief=RAISED)**
2. **mb.grid()**
3. **mb.menu = Menu(mb, tearoff=0)**
4. **mb["menu"] = mb.menu**
5. **xxxVar = IntVar()** - create an integer variable for each button on the menu. Our example requires three variables. A value will be stored in the variable if it is selected.
6. **mb.menu.add_checkbutton(label="xxxxxx", variable=xxxVar)** – add a check button to the list.
   1. label="xxxxxx" - the text that will appear next to the checkbox.
   2. variable=xxxVar – the name of the integer variable that will receive a value if the button is selected.
7. **mb.pack()**

8.13 RadioButton

The RadioButton widget places a radiobutton on the window. A radiobutton is used when there are several possible selections and the user may select only one of the selctions. An example would be when the user is asked to enter the time and then to indicate AM or PM there are two radio buttons.

radbtn.py

```python
#!/usr/bin/python
from Tkinter import *
import Tkinter

def sel():
    selection = "Manufacturer: " + str(var.get())
    label.config(text = selection)

home = Tk()
home.geometry("300x200")
home.title("Demo Radiobutton Widget")

home = Tk()
var = IntVar()
R1 = Radiobutton(home, text="Apple", variable=var, value=1,
                 command=sel)
R1.pack( anchor = W )

R2 = Radiobutton(home, text="Asus", variable=var, value=2,
                 command=sel)
R2.pack( anchor = W )

R3 = Radiobutton(home, text="HP", variable=var, value=3,
                 command=sel)
R3.pack( anchor = W)

R4 = Radiobutton(home, text="Lenovo", variable=var, value=4,
```

```
                    command=sel)
    R4.pack( anchor = W)

    R5 = Radiobutton(home, text="Toshiba", variable=var, value=5,
                    command=sel)
    R5.pack( anchor = W)

    label = Label(home)
    label.pack()

    mainloop()
```

After the line "import tkinter" there is a function that is used later to display
the selection made by the user. The function named sel is:
```
    def sel():
        selection="Manufacturer: " + str(var.get())
        label.config(text=selection)
```
The variable builds a string in a variable named selection that uses a string
literal plus the value returned by the radiobutton selection.

Then after the instruction "home=Tk()" the instructions for the RadioButtons.

1. **var = IntVar()** - this command creates an integer variable named var.
2. **R1=RadioButton(home, text="xxxx", variable=var, value=X, command=sel)** - this
   command creates a RadioButton command in the varaible R1. There will be one
   of these for each radiobutton required.
   1. home - specifies the root window
   2. text="xxxx" - the label text for the radio button.
   3. variable=var - defines the variable where the selection value will be
      stored.
   4. value=X - the value that will be stored if the radiobutton is selected.
      There must be a unique numerical value for each radiobutton.
   5. command=sel - the command that will be executed if the button is selected.
3. **R1=pack(anchor=W)** - This is the second command required to create a
   radiobutton and display it on the window.
4. **label = Label(home)** - defines a label that will display the selected item.
5. **label.pack()**

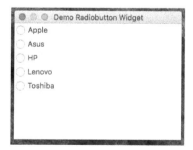

8.14 Summary

These are but a few of the widget choices and attributes. However, the basics of
Python Tkinter are covered here. By no means is this all you can do with Tkinter.

Once you have mastered this lesson, investigate the internet for more information. A Google search will turn up many pages of information and ideas.

Lesson 8 - Quiz

1. Tkinter is the only GUI offered for Python.
a. True
b. False

2. There are _____ ways to place widgets on the window.
a. four
b. three
c. two
d. only one

3. The _____ manager places the widget on a window in the "best fit" location unless directed to a specific location.
a. grid
b. pack
c. widget
d. display

4. The _____ manager places the widgets in a defined cell.
a. grid
b. pack
c. widget
d. display

5. The Label widget can be used to display gif images.
a. True
b. False

6. _____ widgets are used to trigger events.
a. Label
b. Entry
c. Button
d. Spin

7. The _____ widget accepts user input.
a. Text
b. Label
c. Entry
d. Enter

8. The _____ widget allows the programmer to create graphics on the screen.
a. Image
b. Picture
c. Canvas
d. Graphic

9. The _____ widget is used when there are several selections but the user is limited to only one selection.
a. radiobutton
b. checkbox
c. menubox
d. listbox

10.   The _____ widget is used to place a menubar on the window.
a. menubar
b. menu
c. place
d. bar

Lesson 8 - Exercises

Exercise 8.1 Enter your user name and password

Enter the following code in the Python command line.

```
#!/usr/bin/python
from Tkinter import *
import Tkinter
home = Tk()
home.geometry("200x200")
home.title("Template")

cw = 100
ch=170
x=Canvas(home, width=cw, height=ch)
x.pack(anchor='se')

x.create_line(10, 5, 90, 5, fill="#0000ff")
x.create_rectangle(10, 20, 90, 60, fill="#ccffcc")
x.create_oval(10, 100, 90, 150, fill="#ff0000")

mainloop()
```

Now run the program and see examples of lines, circles and rectangles.

Exercise 8.2 On your own

Using what you have learned, write a Python Tkinter program that asks the user to enter a dollar amount for a home loan. Then select a rate from one of 4 rate selections (2.85%; 3.0%; 3.5%; 4.25%) and display the interest on that amount using the percentage selected. The term of the loan is one year.

Interest = Principal * Rate * Term

Exercise 8.3 On your own

Using what you have learned, write a Python Tkinter program that will generate several designs on the screen. Remember there are other geometric figures that can be generated. Do some research and see what you can find.

Lesson 9 - Tkinter Part 2

Objectives:

- Use multiple widgets on a window.
- Use basic Tkinter commands
- Combine basic Tkinter widgets.
- Create simple windows applications using Tkinter widgets.

9.1 Using Tkinter widgets

In the prior lesson we examined some of the basic widgets in Tkinter. The examples were simple and usually only included one widget. In this Lesson we will look at some more advanced code examples. Again, they are not complete applications but ideas to get you started. You will learn more by having a good starting place and then building on that code after doing some research.

This chapter is a "hands-on" chapter. It consists of three programs for you to examine carefully. Then you are given a PROJECT which is a problem to solve using a Python program. The example for the lesson gives you a good start on your program so read it carefully.

9.2 Label, Entry, and Button Combination

This first program demonstrates using the Label Widget, Entry Widget, and Button Widget in a program. This program asks the user to enter a numeric value for feet and then converts feet to meters and displays the result.

<u>**feetcalc.py**</u>

```
#!/usr/bin/python
from Tkinter import *
import Tkinter
import tkMessageBox

home = Tk()
home.geometry("400x200")
home.title("Template")

def do_convert():
  feet_val = float(cvt_from.get())
  meters_val = feet_val * 0.3048
  cvt_to.set('%s meters' % meters_val)

cvt_to=StringVar()
cvt_from=StringVar()
cbox_val=IntVar()

ckb = Button(home, text='Convert', command=do_convert)
lbl=Label(home, text='Convert Feet to Meters: ')
lbl.grid(row=0, column=0, columnspan=2)
from_lbl=Label(home, text='Enter Feet: ')
```

```
from_lbl.grid(row=1, column=0)
from_entry=Entry(home, textvariable=cvt_from)
from_entry.grid(row=1, column=1)
to_lbl=Label(home, text='Result')
to_lbl.grid(row=2, column=0)
result_lbl=Label(home, textvariable=cvt_to)
result_lbl.grid(row=2, column=1)
ckb.grid(row=3, column=0, columnspan=2)
ckb2 = Button(home, text='Quit', command=sys.exit)
ckb2.grid(row=4, column=0, columnspan=2)

def do_convert():
  feet_val = float(cvt_from.get())
  meters_val = feet_val * 0.3048
  cvt_to.set('%s meters' % meters_val)

mainloop()
```

This program produces the following window:

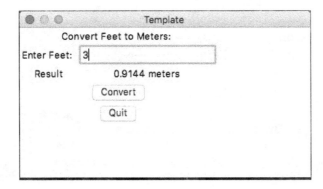

PROJECT:

Using the above example, create a program to convert Fahrenheit temperatures to
Celsius. The formula for the conversion is:

        Celsius = (Fahrenheit - 32) X 5/9
                  OR
        Celsius = (Fahrenheit - 32) / 9/5

Either formula is acceptable. Try both if you want practice. Then find the
formula for conversion of Celsius to Fahrenheit and write the program to do this
conversion.

Then go to the next level and create a program to ask the user which conversion
they would like to do and allow them to choose, enter a value and then show the
result. Practice using both pack and grid managers.

9.3 Working with Color

A little color will dress up a window and used properly can assist the user in finding directions quickly and hopefully lead to a better, more accurate data entry tool.

colorme.py

```
#!/usr/bin/python
from Tkinter import *
import Tkinter

home = Tk()
home.geometry("400x200")
home.title("Template")

msg = StringVar()

def do_color():
  w2 = Label(home, textvariable=msg, fg="white", bg="red")
  w2.pack()

l = Label(home, text="Enter your name: ", fg="green")
l.pack()

inp = Entry(home, textvariable=msg)
inp.pack()

b = Button(home, text="Show", command=do_color)
b.pack()
q = Button(home, text="Quit", command=sys.exit)
q.pack()

mainloop()
```

This program will produce the following window:

PROJECT

Write a Python program that will give the user several menu selections. Each selection will print out a different message in a different color. Remember, changes can include the foreground or the background or both. You may also practice using images as part of your program.

Use any of the other projects in this chapter and add color to make the project more interesting.

9.4 Checkmenu, Radiobuttons and Building Strings

Checkmenus, Radiobuttons are important data entry tools. This program demonstrates using both in the same program. It also demonstrates accumulating the results and constructing a string to display which values were selected by the user.

<u>**hotdog.py**</u>

```python
#!/usr/bin/python
from Tkinter import *
import Tkinter

home = Tk()
home.geometry("600x600")
home.title("Template")

def sel():
   cond = " Toppings: "
   selection = "Served On: " + str(var.get())
   if mustardVar.get() == 1:
     cond = cond + "Mustard "
   if ketchVar.get() == 1:
     cond = cond + "Ketchup "
   if relishVar.get() == 1:
     cond = cond + "Relish "
   if onionVar.get() == 1:
     cond = cond + "Onion"
   lbl02.config(text = selection)
   lbl03.config(text = cond)


l1=Label(home, text="Choose Toppings for your Hot Dog", fg="blue")
l1.pack()

mb=  Menubutton (home, text="Toppings", relief=RAISED )
mb.grid()
mb.menu  =  Menu (mb, tearoff = 0 )
mb["menu"]  =  mb.menu

mustardVar  = IntVar()
ketchVar = IntVar()
relishVar = IntVar()
onionVar = IntVar()

mb.menu.add_checkbutton ( label="mustard",
                          variable=mustardVar )
mb.menu.add_checkbutton ( label="ketchup",
                          variable=ketchVar )
mb.menu.add_checkbutton ( label="relish",
                          variable=relishVar )
mb.menu.add_checkbutton ( label="onion",
                          variable=onionVar )

mb.pack()

rlbl = Label(home, text="Do you want Hot Dog on:", fg="blue")
rlbl.pack()
```

```
var = StringVar()
R1 = Radiobutton(home, text="Bun", variable=var, value="Bun",
                 command=sel)
R1.pack( anchor = W )

R2 = Radiobutton(home, text="Wheat Bun", variable=var, value="Wheat Bun",
                 command=sel)
R2.pack( anchor = W )

R3 = Radiobutton(home, text="No Bun", variable=var, value="No Bun",
                 command=sel)
R3.pack( anchor = W)

lbl02 = Label(home)
lbl02.pack()
lbl03 = Label(home)
lbl03.pack()

btn = Button(home, text="Order", command=sys.exit)
btn.pack()
mainloop()
```

This program will produce the following window:

PROJECT

You are going to purchase a car. Write a program that will allow you to select
from three different models: SE, LE, XLE. Then select from a list of options.
Options could be: Premium Radio, Remote Start, Trim Package, Leather Seats, Sport
Package, Tire Package. After the user has made selections, display the choices on
the window.

9.5 Summary

This lesson has given some example code and then allowed the learner to create
another similar program. The last two chapters have just touched on the use of
widgets. There are other widgets and other attributes that will make your Python
windows better and more professional. Learn the basics and then investigate some
of the advanced options.

APPENDIX

Start Programming with Python

Practice Programming Projects

The best way to learn any programming language is to write programs. This section provides ideas for projects for you to program. See how many of these projects you can solve with what you have learned. Read each one carefully and plan your approach to solve the problem. These are all business / personal type projects from everyday problems.

```
Project 1   - Lumber
Project 2   - Planet Weight
Project 3   - Dog Years
Project 4   - Coins Weight & Thickness
Project 5   - Mortgage Calculator
Project 6   - Change Maker
Project 7   - Currency Converter
```

Some of the project give you sample input and output, others do not. These exercises are for you to learn to program AND to do the design.

Some programs can be done several different ways. I highly recommend that you learn to write this program several different ways. Explore different ways to write the various programs. Enhance the programs, add functionality, always try to make your program do more than the original design. Try things and if you wreck your program, I hope you learn something like what NOT to do in a program. This is software, you can't break anything.

Project 1 - Lumber

The standard 2″ x 4″ board is not 2 inches by 4 inches. It may start that way but by the time the process is finished in producing the board it winds up smaller. Write a program that asks the user to select the lumber dimension and then displays the actual size in inches and metric. Use the following table for values:

Nominal	Actual	Metric
1″ x 2″	3/4″ x 1-1/2″	19 x 38 mm
1″ x 3″	3/4″ x 2-1/2″	19 x 64 mm
1″ x 4″	3/4″ x 3-1/2″	19 x 89 mm
1″ x 5″	3/4″ x 4-1/2″	19 x 114 mm
1″ x 6″	3/4″ x 5-1/2″	19 x 140 mm
1″ x 7″	3/4″ x 6-1/4″	19 x 159 mm
1″ x 8″	3/4″ x 7-1/4″	19 x 184 mm
1″ x 10″	3/4″ x 9-1/4″	19 x 235 mm
1″ x 12″	3/4″ x 11-1/4″	19 x 286 mm
2″ x 4″	1-1/2″ x 3-1/2″	38 x 89 mm
2″ x 6″	1-1/2″ x 5-1/2″	38 x 140 mm
2″ x 8″	1-1/2″ x 7-1/4″	38 x 184 mm
2″ x 10″	1-1/2″ x 9-1/4″	38 x 235 mm
2″ x 12″	1-1/2″ x 11-1/4″	38 x 286 mm
3″ x 6″	2-1/2″ x 5-1/2″	64 x 140 mm
4″ x 4″	3-1/2″ x 3-1/2″	89 x 89 mm
4″ x 6″	3-1/2″ x 5-1/2″	89 x 140 mm

This program can be done two different ways.

Project 2 - Planet Weight

The effects of gravity on various planets will affect your weight. Using Earth weight as our baseline for our weight, create a program that will ask for the users weight on earth and then determine the weight value for each of the other planets.

Planet	Multiply By
Mercury	0.37
Venus	0.88
Mars	0.38
Jupiter	2.64
Saturn	1.20
Neptune	1.12
Uranus	1.15
Pluto	0.04

SAMPLE INPUT

       Enter the Weight on Earth: **189**

SAMPLE OUTPUT

       Weight on Earth   189
       Weight on Mercury   xxx
       Weight on Venus   xxx
       Weight on Mars   xxx
       Weight on Jupiter   xxx
       Weight on Saturn   xxx
       Weight on Neptune   xxx
       Weight on Uranus   xxx
       Weight on Pluto   xxx

This program can be done two different ways. Use arrays or put the information in a MySQL database. I highly recommend that you learn to write this program both ways.

Project 3 - Dog Years Converter

This program will calculate the number of months alive, given the years and the months old. The user enters the age in years and months and the program calculates and displays the number of months alive. Then calculates the age in dog years and displays that information also.

SAMPLE INPUT:

Age in Years: **15**
Months since last birthday: **3**

User enters 15 for years and 3 for months.

SAMPLE OUTPUT:

You are 183 months old

In Dog years your age is 76.3 years old.

Project 4 - Coins - Weight

You have saved coins in a big jar. Now it is time to cash in. Counting all those coin will be a big pain but you want to have some idea how much you have saved before going to the bank. You researched the weight of coins and found the following table on the internet.

Denomination	Weight	Thickness
$0.01	2.500 grams	1.52 millimeters
$0.05	5.000 grams	1.95 millimeters
$0.10	2.268 grams	1.35 millimeters
$0.25	5.670 grams	1.75 millimeters
$0.50	11.340 grams	2.15 millimeters
$1.00	8.1 grams	2.00 millimeters

You decide to sort your coins by denomination and then weigh the pennies, nickels, dimes, quarters, half-dollars, and dollars and use their weight and the above table to calculate the approximate value of the coins.

Write a program that asks the user for the denomination, the total weight of the coins of that denomination, and the program calculates how many coins and their approximate value. The program displays the value of the coins and asks for the next denomination. When the user quits the program, a table is displayed with the denomination, the number of coins, and the value. The program will also display the total value of all the coins.
NOTE: Multiply Ounces by 28 to get Grams.

Coins - Stacks
You have saved coins in a big jar. Now it is time to cash in. Counting all those coin will be a big pain but you want to have some idea how much you have saved before going to the bank. You researched the thickness of coins and found the following table on the internet.

Denomination	Weight	Thickness
$0.01	2.500 grams	1.52 millimeters
$0.05	5.000 grams	1.95 millimeters
$0.10	2.268 grams	1.35 millimeters
$0.25	5.670 grams	1.75 millimeters
$0.50	11.340 grams	2.15 millimeters
$1.00	8.1 grams	2.00 millimeters

You decide to sort your coins by denomination and then measure the stacks of the pennies, nickels, dimes, quarters, half-dollars, and dollars and use their thickness and the above table to calculate the approximate value of the coins.

Write a program that asks the user for the denomination, the height of the stack of the coins of that denomination, and the program calculates how many coins and their approximate value. The program displays the value of the coins and asks for the next denomination. When the user quits the program, a table is displayed with the denomination, the number of coins, and the value. The program will also display the total value of all the coins.
NOTE: Divide Inches by 0.039370 to get Millimeters.

This program can be done two different ways. Use arrays or put the information in a MySQL database. I highly recommend that you learn to write this program both ways.

Project 5 - Mortgage Calculator

Write a program to calculate the Monthly Payment for a mortgage using the following information:
    Principal Amount
    Interest Rate
    Term (length of loan 30 years, 20 years, 10 years)

Use the Formula:
    Monthly Payment = Principal * MonthInt / (1-(1/(1+MonthInt)) ^ (Years * 12))

        MonthInt = Interest Rate / 12

The user enters the information into a form. Enter the Principal Amount in Dollars and Cents, the Interest Rate as a decimal (EXAMPLE: 3.95% entered as .0395) and the term which can be 30 years, 20 years or 10 years. The program should validate the data in all three entries.

The Monthly Payment should be calculated and displayed as shown below.

SAMPLE OUTPUT:

Amount Borrowed:	$100000
Interest Rate:	3.95%
Term:	30
Monthly Payment:	$000.00

Project 6 - Change Maker

Develop a program that allows the user to enter a sale amount between $0.01 and $99.99. Then ask for a payment amount between $0.01 and $100.00. Then ask the user for the change due. The program should calculate the change due and if the user entered the correct amount, display the users estimate, the actual amount and if they match print "CORRECT!". If the amounts do not match print the message "TRY AGAIN!".

SAMPLE INPUT:

Amount of Sale:	**79.59**
Cash Tendered:	**100.00**
Estimated Change Due:	**21.41**

SAMPLE OUTPUT:

Your estimate was	21.41	
Actual	21.41	
	CORRECT!	Or if not correct: TRY AGAIN!

Then ask the user how many of each denomination should be returned in change. Denominations of $50; $20; $10; $5; $1; $0.50; $0.25; $0.10; $0.05; and $0.01 may be used. The program should calculate the optimum denominations to make the change and compare to what the user selected. If a match, Congratulations, if not a match, TRY AGAIN!

SAMPLE INPUT

$50	0
$20	1
$10	0
$5	0
$1	1
$0.50	0
$0.25	1
$0.10	1
$0.05	1
$0.01	1

SAMPLE OUTPUT

AMOUNT: 21.41

Denomination	You	Computer
$50	0	0
$20	1	1
$10	0	0
$5	0	0
$1	1	1
$0.50	0	0
$0.25	1	1
$0.10	1	1
$0.05	1	1
$0.01	1	1

CORRECT!

Project 7 - Currency Converter

Write a program that asks for a whole dollar amount from the user and select the foreign currency from a list. Then does a currency conversion from US Dollars entered to the currency selected. Use the following table for conversion factors.

Currency	Conversion Factor
Euro	0.730
English Pound	0.595
Japanese Yen	101.545
Russian Ruble	34.745
Mexican Peso	12.893
Canadian Dollar	1.086
Korean Won	1,024.100
Norwegian Krone	5.934

Some variations to this program are:
1. Put the table in an array.
2. Put the table in a file.
3. Convert from the foreign currency to US Dollars.
4. Select a from currency and a to currency and convert.
5. Get additional conversion factors and include more currencies.

Python Editors and IDEs

IDLE

The Integrated DeveLopment Environment (IDLE) is written in Python using the Tkinter GUI. It is fully supported on Windows, Linux and Mac OS/X platforms. It is an interactive interpreter and assists the programmer by colorizing code as it is input, output and errors. Also supports search and replace as well as a debugger feature.

The official site: www.python.org

PyCharm

"All Python Tools in One Place"

A Python IDE with many features to allow the programmer to be more productive. Code completion, error checking, project navigation and more. Designed to help the programmer write maintainable code and offers good testing assistance. Advertised as 'Developed by programmers for programmers."

Pycharm supports autocomplete, and syntax highlighting for various programming languages.

Pycharm was released in 2010.

The official site: jetbrains.com

Sublime Text

A commercial text editor that has been around since 2008. It is a fast and powerful tex code editor that supports a wide array of programming languages including Python.

The official site:

Notepad++

A free open-source code editor for windows. It is a small and fast editor that has many features like, sytax highlighting, autocompletion, multi document(a tab interface), zoom, multi language and much more.

The official site: https://notepad-plus-plus.org

TextWrangler - Version 4.5.10

A powerful, general purpose text editor. Features syntax coloring and function navigation for Python and many other code languages. Written for Mac OS/X 10.8.5 or later.

TextWrangler allows you to test your Python scripts in TextWrangler by selecting the Run in Terminal option from the menubar.

There is a online manual of 258 pages.

The official site for TextWrangler: Www.barebones.com

Smultron - Version 3.5.1

Created, designed and programmed by Peter Borg. A text editor wirtten in Cocoa for Mac OS/X Leopard 10.5 both powerful and easy to use. Smultron can be used to create or edit any text document. Supports syntax colors for over 100 code languages. Can be used for scripts, HTML or just text files.

Smultron help is a 46 page Reference amanual.

The official site for Smultron: www.peterborgapps.com

IronPython

Advertised on the site as: "An open-source implementation of the Python programming language which is tightly integrated with the .NET framework. IronPython can use the .NET framework and Python Libraries and other .NET languages can use Python code just as easily."

BlueFish Editor

A powerful editor for programmers and web developers. BludFish supports many programming and markup languages. It is open-source under GNU and GPL. Multi-Platform supported by Linux, Windows and Mac OS/X. Some of the features are, unlimited undo/redo, lightweight and fast, multiple document interface and Project Support.

The official site: bluefish.openoffice.nl

Others

There are many other text editors and IDE's sutible for use with Python. This is just a sampling of the many available. Try a few and make up your own mind which tool fits best the way you work.

NOTES

NOTES

www.ingramcontent.com/pod-product-compliance
Lightning Source LLC
Chambersburg PA
CBHW060448060326

40689CB00020B/4475